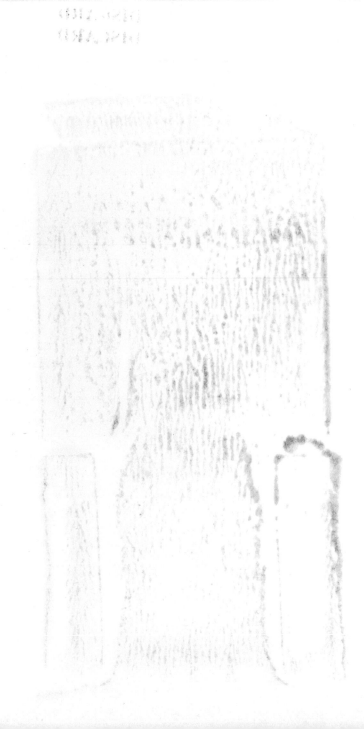

FURTHER EXPLORATIONS

By the same Author

★

DRAMA AND SOCIETY IN THE AGE OF JOHNSON
EXPLORATIONS
SOME SHAKESPEAREAN THEMES
AN APPROACH TO HAMLET

FURTHER EXPLORATIONS

By

L. C. KNIGHTS

King Edward VII Professor of English Literature
in the University of Cambridge

STANFORD UNIVERSITY PRESS
STANFORD, CALIFORNIA

Stanford University Press
Stanford, California
© 1965 by L. C. Knights
Original edition 1965
Reprinted 1966

Printed in the United States of America

To

my colleagues in the Department

of English, Bristol University,

1953–1964

ACKNOWLEDGMENTS

The essays in this volume were written for a variety of purposes during the last twenty years. With one exception they were originally delivered as lectures—a fact that I have not troubled to disguise. 'Poetry, Politics, and the English Tradition' (1953), my inaugural lecture as Winterstoke Professor of English at Bristol, was published by Chatto and Windus. 'Shakespeare's Politics', the Annual Shakespeare Lecture of the British Academy for 1957, was published in Volume XLIII of the *Proceedings* of the Academy (Oxford University Press). 'Personality and Politics in *Julius Caesar*' was read in the Mid-day Series at the Students' Union in the University of Pittsburgh, 1962, and has appeared in the Shakespeare Quatercentenary number of *Anglica* (Japan). 'The Strange Case of Christopher Marlowe' (1964) was prepared at the invitation of the Master and Fellows of Corpus Christi College, Cambridge, as a contribution to the Marlowe Quatercentenary Celebrations of the College, and was delivered at the opening of the Lady Mitchell Memorial Hall. 'The Social Background of Metaphysical Poetry', read to the Doughty Society of Downing College, was published in *Scrutiny*, Vol. XIII, No. 1, Spring, 1945. 'Reflections on Clarendon's *History of the Rebellion*', read to the Cambridge University English Club, was published in *Scrutiny*, Vol. XV, No. 2, Spring, 1948. 'Historical Scholarship and the Interpretation of Shakespeare' appeared in the *Sewanee Review*, Vol. LXIII, No. 2, Spring, 1955. 'Idea and Symbol: Some Hints from Coleridge', a contribution to the Twelfth Symposium of the Colston Research Society, Bristol, 1960, was published in Volume XII of the *Proceedings* of the Society, *Metaphor and Symbol*, edited by L. C. Knights and Basil Cottle (Butterworths Scientific Publications London). '*King Lear* as Metaphor' was read to a joint meeting

ACKNOWLEDGMENTS

of the Midwest Modern Language Association and the Central Renaissance Conference, held at the University of Nebraska in April, 1962: with other papers delivered at the meeting it was published in *Myth and Symbol: Critical Approaches and Applications*, edited by Bernice Slote (Bison Books; University of Nebraska Press). 'The Question of Character in Shakespeare', a lecture delivered at one of the Shakespeare Memorial Theatre's Summer Schools, was published in *More Talking of Shakespeare*, edited by John Garrett (Longmans, 1959). I am glad to make acknowledgment to all concerned for permission to reprint.

L. C. K.

Bristol University,
June, 1964.

CONTENTS

9

Shakespeare's Politics: with Some Reflections on the Nature of Tradition

AS my rather cumbersome title indicates, this lecture is an attempt to bring together two interests—an interest in the nature of Shakespeare's political wisdom, and an interest in the nature of tradition. Shakespeare, as is proper, will get most of the attention, but I should like to begin by indicating the wider concern. There is no need to emphasize the importance for us in these days of an understanding of the nature of a living tradition. It is something which literary studies and studies in the background of literature should foster. But there are two dangers that—it seems to me—are insufficiently guarded against. There is the danger of allowing the 'background' metaphor to dominate our thinking. We need to think in terms of promptings and incitements to decent living and clear thought, rather than in terms of assumptions that are merely accepted and taken for granted, which is what 'background' tends to suggest. The second danger is inherent in the increased availability of information about a past age. One result of the accumulation of 'background' studies—even of necessary and valuable studies—is to suggest that what was peculiar to an age, what can only now be recovered by thinking our way into past systems of thought, is what we most need to know if we are to enter fully into the imaginative achievements of that age. Certainly we need, at times and according to our capacities, to make ourselves into Elizabethans, and to think in terms like those that Dr Tillyard, for example, has made generally available in *The Elizabethan World Picture*. But I sometimes suspect that in concentrating on what was peculiar to the age, on categories of thought that can only be reconstructed by an effort of the historical imagination, we are in danger of losing sight

11

of something even more important. May it not be that what was most nourishing of creative achievement in the past was what, in the tradition of the time, is—or should be—most available for us now? It is towards some understanding of one aspect of tradition in the sixteenth century—the promptings, namely, that lie behind Shakespeare's individual approach to political issues—that this inquiry is directed. I use the word 'directed' deliberately: neither the time at my disposal nor my own severely limited equipment will allow me to do much more than to lead up to the questions that I should like to see answered.

i

When we speak of Shakespeare's politics there are possibilities of misunderstanding to guard against. 'Policy', 'politic', and 'politician' are words that occur in Shakespeare, sometimes with a pejorative implication—'a scurvy politician', 'base and rotten policy'—that might tempt us to suppose a context like that of the modern political platform. The supposition would of course be wrong. 'Politics' (which Shakespeare does not use) only acquired its most frequent modern meanings—'political affairs', 'political principles or opinions'—much later, with the rise of the parties. If you had said to Shakespeare, 'Do you take any part in politics?' or 'What are your politics?' he would probably have been puzzled. 'Politics' still implied systematic thought on the constitution of states and the art of government —a matter for philosophers: our 'politics', the conduct of internal affairs of state, together with the observation of 'who's in, who's out', and plans to reverse that order—these were matters for the men who did the work, of constant interest only to them, to those with special interests to press, and to a fringe of Politic Would-be's. Shakespeare, like the great majority of his fellow-countrymen, 'had no politics': he had too many other things to think about. The fact remains, however, that although he made no arbitrary separation between what is politics and what is not (and this, to anticipate, is a notable aspect of his political wisdom), he showed throughout his career a lively concern with men not only in their private and personal, but in their public and formal, relations. And this concern included questions of power and subordination, of mutual relations within a constituted society, of the ends and methods of public action, so that we may properly speak of Shakespeare's political philosophy—so long, that is, as we remember that this philosophy is not something ready formed once for all, and applied or exhibited in varying circumstances, but a part of that constant search for meanings that informs his work as a whole.

A recent writer on the history of political thought has called Shakespeare 'a superb interpreter of group psychology and an almost unrivalled observer of political behaviour'.[1] I doubt whether these phrases quite do justice to Shakespeare's political wisdom. They do, however, call attention to one element in it, namely its realism. Shakespeare's political realism is not of course Machiavellian or modern realism ('How realistic is the realist?' is a question that the plays force us to ask), but it is certainly based on a clear perception of the actualities of political situations. Consider for example the implicit comment made by the play *Richard II* on the wishful thinking of a king for whom words and dramatic postures take the place of action; the explicit comments of the Bastard on 'commodity' in *King John*, and the place his comments have within the larger political action; or the sombre demonstration in *King Henry IV* of

[1] Christopher Morris, *Political Thought in England: Tyndale to Hooker* (H.U.L.), p. 103.

13

what is involved in getting and keeping power: the recognition
of inevitable consequences by the dying Bolingbroke

—For all my reign hath been but as a scene
Acting that argument—

enforces the same political moral as Marvell's Horatian Ode

—The same Arts that did gain
A Power must it maintain—

and enforces it with a similar effect of irony. But Shakespeare's
realism goes further than this; fundamentally it is a refusal to
allow the abstract and general to obscure the personal and
specific. After the earliest plays on English history Shakespeare's
political plays are not shaped by a predetermined pattern of
ideas: like the rest of his work they are the result of a full exposure to experience. If they unavoidably raise moral issues it is
because of the felt pressure of life itself.[1] If they clarify for us
Clarendon's phrase about 'that fathomless abyss of Reason of
State', it is because they insist on setting every 'political' action
in the widest possible human context and so—implicitly, if not
always explicitly—assessing it in relation to that context. It is of
especial significance that the political action of *Henry IV* has for
setting scenes in which the actions of great ones take on a quite
different appearance, in which the assumptions of the dominant
groups are by no means taken for granted, and which therefore
act as a challenge to those assumptions.

In the two political plays that follow *Henry IV*, in *Henry V*
and *Julius Caesar*, Shakespeare continues the questioning of what
statesmen are likely to accept without question. It is one of the
curiosities of literature that *Henry V* should have been seen so
often as a simple glorification of the hero-king. I am not suggest-

---

[1] I have in mind the passage in Henry James's Preface to *The Portrait of a
Lady*, where he speaks of 'the perfect dependence of the "moral" sense of a
work of art on the amount of felt life concerned in producing it'.

ing that we should merely reverse the conventional estimate. It is simply that, on the evidence of the play itself, Shakespeare's attitude towards the King is complex and critical. As M. Fluchère has said, 'While making the necessary concessions to patriotic feeling ... Shakespeare lets us see ... that the political problem, linked with the moral problem, is far from being solved by a victorious campaign and a marriage with happy consequences for the country.'[1] In other words, the political problem, purely at the level of politics and the political man, is insoluble. In *Julius Caesar*, freed from the embarrassments of a patriotic theme, and with the problem projected into a 'Roman' setting, Shakespeare examines more closely the contradictions and illusions involved in political action. The matter cannot be properly argued here, but it seems to me undeniable that the play offers a deliberate contrast between the person and the public persona, the face and the mask; that tragic illusion and error are shown to spring from the wrenching apart of the two worlds—the personal and the public; and that Brutus, in particular, is a study in what Coleridge was to describe as the politics of pure—or abstract—reason, with the resulting sophistries and inevitable disappointments.[2]

I hope that even from so cursory a survey of some of the plays preceding the great tragedies one point has become clear: that even in plays where the political interest is most evident, it is never exclusive or, as it were, self-contained. The implied question, What does this political action or attitude mean? is invariably reduced to personal terms: How does this affect relations between men? What kind of man acts in this way? How does he further make himself by so acting? Swift says of

[1] Henri Fluchère, *Shakespeare*, p. 204. I also agree with Mr D. A. Traversi that the effect of the play is 'to bring out certain contradictions, moral and human, inherent in the notion of a successful king'. *Shakespeare: from 'Richard II' to 'Henry V'*, p. 177.

[2] See *The Friend*, First Section, 'On the Principles of Political Knowledge'.

the party man, 'when he is got near the walls of his assembly he assumes and affects an entire set of very different airs; he conceives himself a being of a superior nature to those without, and acting in a sphere, where the vulgar methods for the conduct of human life can be of no use.'[1] It is Shakespeare's distinction that, when dealing with rulers and matters of state, he constantly brings us back to 'the vulgar methods for the conduct of human life', that he refuses to accept a closed realm of the political. Indeed, it is only by a deliberate focusing of our interest for a particular purpose that we can separate 'political' from 'non-political' plays, the two kinds being in fact linked by common themes and preoccupations. Thus in the Second Part of *Henry IV* Shakespeare's interests are plainly setting away from his ostensible subject towards a more fundamental exploration of the human condition that points towards the great tragedies; and *Julius Caesar* shares with later, non-political plays, a preoccupation with the ways in which men give themselves to illusion. So too, from *Julius Caesar* onwards, it is possible to trace Shakespeare's political themes only in plays that, with the exception of *Coriolanus*, are not primarily political plays.

Troilus and Cressida, King Lear, Macbeth—each of these, in one of its aspects, takes the political theme a stage further. *Troilus and Cressida* makes a simple but far-reaching discovery: it is that the sixteenth-century commonplace of the necessity for order and degree might mean much or little according as the reason that formulated it was, or was not, grounded in the responsiveness to life of the whole person. I refer especially to what might be called the dramatic status of Ulysses' well-known speech on 'degree'. In the context of the whole play—the clash of varied attitudes to life which forces us to a judgment—this speech appears as something other than the expression of an

---

[1] Swift is speaking of 'those, who in a late reign began the distinction between the personal and politick capacity'. *A Discourse of the Contests . . . between the Nobles and the Commons in Athens and Rome* (1701), chap. V.

unquestioned standard: for the significant thing is that it is spoken by Ulysses, and Ulysses is the chief exponent of a reason and policy that do not, any more than Troilus' emotionalism, commend themselves to us. To put it simply, just as emotion, divorced from reason, is reduced to appetite ('And the will dotes that is inclinable To what infectiously itself affects . . .'), so reason, divorced from intuition, is reduced to cleverness: statecraft, for Ulysses, is the manipulation of men. Political order and authority—so the play as a whole forces us to conclude—are not concepts to be accepted without question, independent of some prior ground from which they draw their justification.

That ground is explored in *King Lear*; it is taken for granted in *Macbeth* and *Coriolanus*. What I mean is this. *King Lear* is not a political play; it is a play about the conditions of being human, and it seeks to answer the great question put by Lear as Everyman, 'Who is it that can tell me who I am?' But at the same time it has marked political implications. A play in which 'the king *is* but as the beggar' was bound to raise the social question, and to do rather more than hint that 'distribution should undo excess'. It was almost bound to raise the question of justice: why should the half-witted vagrant be whipped from tithing to tithing, or the farmer's dog be an image of authority? But the political implications go further than that. In a lecture on 'The Politics of *King Lear*' Edwin Muir has suggested that Goneril, Regan, and Edmund have in common a way of seeing people which lacks a dimension. For Edmund, as A. C. Bradley had remarked, men and women are 'divested of all quality except their relation to [his] end; as indifferent as mathematical quantities or mere physical agents'. So too, says Mr Muir, Goneril and Regan 'exist in this shallow present'; without memory, they are without responsibility, and their speech 'consists of a sequence of pitiless truisms. . . . Their shallowness is ultimately that of the Machiavellian view of life as it was understood in [Shakespeare's] age, of "policy". . . . We need not shrink from regarding Edmund and his confederates as political types'.[1] This, if we do not push it too far, suggests one of the ways in which the group opposed to Lear may properly be regarded. And the converse also holds. *King Lear* establishes the grounds of any politics that claim to be more than a grammar of power. Behind hierarchy and authority, behind formal justice and public order, is a community of persons bound by 'holy cords. . . . Which are too intrinse t'unloose'. The basic political facts of this play are that men can feel for each other, and that this directness of relationship—expressing itself in the humblest of ways as well as in the most exalted forms of loyalty and sacrifice—is the only alternative to a predatory power-seeking whose necessary end is anarchy. Ulysses, it will be remembered, had foretold how chaos would follow the 'choking' of degree:

> Then everything includes itself in power,
> Power into will, will into appetite;
> And appetite, an universal wolf,
> So doubly seconded with will and power,
> Must make perforce an universal prey,
> And last eat up himself.

In *King Lear*, Albany, envisaging the same state of chaos, significantly shifts the argument:

> That nature, which contemns it origin,
> Cannot be border'd certain in itself;
> She that herself will sliver and disbranch
> From her material sap, perforce must wither
> And come to deadly use . . .

[1] 'The Politics of *King Lear*', *Essays in Literature and Society*, pp. 39–42. See also J. F. Danby's *Shakespeare's Doctrine of Nature: a Study of 'King Lear'*, especially, in this connexion, p. 38.

If that the heavens do not their visible spirits
Send quickly down to tame these vile offences,
It will come,
Humanity must perforce prey on itself,
Like monsters of the deep.

We hardly need to put each passage back in its context to see
that the later one draws on a far deeper sense of what it is that
sanctions the human order.[1] Lear's discovery of his kinship with
the naked poor is both a moral and a political discovery: it is a
king who says, 'O! I have ta'en too little care of this.

That is what I meant by saying that *Macbeth* takes for granted
the ground established in *King Lear*. Evil in *Macbeth* is more than
tyranny; but tyranny is part of the evil, and it is defined in
terms of a violation of those bonds—the 'holy cords'—that are
essential to the being of man as man. We cannot fail to be
affected by the varied images of concord, of mutual service and
relationship, through which we are made aware that behind the
disintegration and dissolution of Macbeth's state—of his 'single
state of man' and of the state at large—are contrasting possibilities of order. And it seems to me that the conception of
order—as we are given it, in the play—draws on a different
dimension of experience from that envisaged in the 'degree'
speech of Ulysses. In *Macbeth* institutional life—all that is indicated and symbolized by churches, castles, 'humane statute'—
guards and guarantees a living system of relationships ('honour,
love, obedience . . .'), which in turn are related to more than
human sanctions. Thus the evocation of the temple-haunting

[1] In *The Allegory of Love* (p. 110) C. S. Lewis translates some lines from
the Latin *Architrenius* of Johannes de Altavilla which curiously sum up the
central movement of *King Lear*, including its political meaning:

> This must I do—go exil'd through the world
> And seek for Nature till far hence I find
> Her secret dwelling-place; there drag to light
> The hidden cause of quarrel, and reknit,
> Haply reknit, the long-divided Love.

martlets, of the birds that securely build and breed, is an image of life delighting in life, and it subtly and powerfully contributes to our sense of the ideal presence of a life-bearing order in the human commonwealth—in what the play calls 'the gentle weal'.[1]

In *Coriolanus*, which is the last of the great tragedies and also the last overtly political play, Shakespeare takes up again from the earlier 'histories' the theme of the Governor. Those earlier plays were largely, though not exclusively, studies of rulers who failed because they were isolated within an arbitrary conception of power or privilege: and I think one could deduce from them that Shakespeare saw the good ruler as not merely set over the people whom he ruled (though rule is necessary), but linked with, and in some sense expressive of, the society for whose sake he performs his office.[2] In *Coriolanus* the main subject is the relation between a member of the ruling class, a Governor, and the political society to which he belongs; and the handling of it results in a breaking-down of any over-simple distinction we might be tempted to make between what is 'individual', on the one hand, and what is 'social' and 'political' on the other. It is clear that if individual qualities are partly the result of social pressures (behind Coriolanus is Volumnia, and behind Volumnia is the patrician class), the political crisis is, to say the least, exacerbated by the personal disorders that play into it. The isolation and over-development of one quality in

[1] These values are of course positively present to our minds and imaginations even in the explicit denial of them by the protagonists—in Macbeth's great invocation of chaos in IV, i, for example.

[2] In the simple moralizing of the gardeners' scene in *Richard II* (III, iv) the King's function is explicitly to 'trim and dress' his land, 'as we this garden': that is, not to impose his mere will, but to foster what is given in accordance with the laws of its nature. We may compare Burgundy's speech in *Henry V*, V, ii. In *Measure for Measure* Escalus, unlike Angelo—and this helps to define the Deputy—has a side of himself open to the rather foolish Elbow: Angelo talks about abstract justice; Escalus patiently sifts the evidence in an apparently unimportant case.

the hero is not only analogous to the failure of connexion and integration in the social group ('Rome and her rats'), the one is shown as having a direct bearing on the other. The play thus draws on the same established affirmations as *Macbeth*: the state is not simply an embodiment of power, it is society in its political or public aspect; and society is a mutual relation of persons who, by and large, need each other if they are to come to anything like maturity. What the play emphasizes is the challenge of difference and diversity. There is no suggestion that the social distinctions between patricians and plebeians ought not to exist: it *is* suggested that the diversified social group, the body politic, is in danger of corruption to the extent that *what lies behind diversity* is lost sight of. 'What lies behind' is of course simple humanity. It is Coriolanus's defective humanity that makes him a defective governor.

If I have spoken as though these plays offered us a simple political moral or message, my excuse must be that the necessary qualifications are sufficiently obvious. Indeed it might be claimed that my simplifications have all been in the interest of a recognition of complexity. Shakespeare's political thought, I have insisted, is not a body of abstract principles to be applied and illustrated. It is part of a continuous exploration and assessment of experience: it grows and develops. And in any one play it is part of a complex organization whose very nature it is, as work of art, to challenge each individual reader to become imaginatively alive: the political meanings are only *there* to the extent that we do so respond. So long as we keep this clearly in mind, simplification may have its uses. What I most want to suggest, then, is that Shakespeare's political meanings—the things he tells us about politics—are inherent in and inseparable from his method, his way of presenting his political material. Aware as he is of the need for mutual relationships within society, he does not merely preach this: rather he explores— with a maximum of concreteness and immediacy—the nature of mutuality and its opposite. Thus the distrust that he shows, from first to last, for individualism—for the attitude expressed in Richard of Gloucester's 'I am myself alone'—is based on a sure grasp of the self-mutilation inherent in egotism and isolation, of the inevitable denaturing effect of an attitude that wilfully blinds itself to the fact that personal life only has its being in relationship: Macbeth as tyrant inevitably 'keeps alone'. The converse of this is the pervasive sense that we find in the plays that the foundations of political organization are in the realm 'beyond politics', in those varied relationships that are the necessary condition of individual growth: it is only a Caliban (and Caliban drunk at that) who can wish for an untrammelled 'freedom'. What we may call the idea of the state in Shakespeare is thus fundamentally opposed to the Renaissance conception of the state as a work of art.[1] Nor can it be adequately expressed by the conventional analogy of the bees,

> Creatures that by a rule in nature teach
> The act of order to a peopled kingdom.

Shakespeare probed further and more subtly than the political Archbishop of *Henry V*. What he went on to ask—what, I think, he was already asking when he wrote *Henry V*—was, what are the foundations of a living order? Both *Macbeth* and *Coriolanus* confirm the maxims,

> If a man have not order within him
> He can not spread order about him . . .
> And if the prince have not order within him
> He can not put order in his dominions:

the disordered man makes for disorder, not only in his more

---

[1] See Burckhardt, *The Civilization of the Renaissance*, Part I, 'The State as a Work of Art'.

immediate circle but in his wider social relations.¹ And the contrasting positive values? Shakespeare does not sum things up for us, but I think that a few sentences from Boethius' *De Consolatione Philosophiae* (in the English of Chaucer) come close to the spirit of his political philosophy: '. . . al this accordaunce of thynges is bounde with love, that governeth erthe and see, and hath also commandement to the hevene. . . . This love halt togidres peples joyned with an holy boond, . . . and love enditeth lawes to trewe felawes.'² The love that is in question is not of course simply a matter of feeling; it includes a neighbourly tolerance of differences and a sense of mutual need; and in its openness to life, its willingness to *listen*, it is allied to that justice which gives each man his due, looking towards what he is, or can become; and there is delight superadded.³ Shakespeare's abundance, his feeling for uniqueness and variety, his imaginative grasp of what makes for life—these qualities ensure that when political issues are handled in the plays we sense behind them a concern for the 'trewe felawes' (Boethius' *sodales*), for the living body politic in all its variety. We are inevitably prompted to a clearer recognition of the fact that a wholesome political order is not something arbitrary and imposed, but an expression of relationships between particular persons within an organic society. The 'concord' that Shakespeare invokes as

¹ Ezra Pound (Canto XIII) puts these words into the mouth of a Chinese sage. The idea, I suppose, is common in Western philosophy; my point is that Shakespeare does not merely invoke the idea, valuable as it is, he makes vividly present the kind of actuality from which the idea springs. Professor D. W. Harding, writing on the psychological aspects of war in *The Impulse to Dominate*, has reminded us that a mass phenomenon like war is not something that simply *happens* to a community, that in the last analysis it is rooted in individual habits that make part of the texture of normal 'peaceful' existence.

² Book II, Metrum 8.

³ Paul Tillich's *Love, Power and Justice*, describing the intrinsic and necessary relation between these three concepts, will be found to clarify the meaning of love in social—as well as in directly personal—relations. On listening as a function of creative justice see especially pp. 84-5.

the alternative to both tyranny and anarchy in *Macbeth*[1] has
this depth of meaning behind it.

ii

In this last part of my lecture I want to look beyond Shakespeare and to ask some questions. None of Shakespeare's greater
plays can be adequately 'explained' by anything outside itself;
each is its unique self, with its own virtually inexhaustible
depth of meaning—'so ramm'd with life It can but gather
strength of life with being'. But no work of art, above all no
major work, is entirely original: promptings and insights from
the past have helped to make it, so that to apprehend it is in
some measure to apprehend them. Shakespeare, undoubtedly,
was receptive to what his age had to offer, and we have had
valuable studies showing his awareness of the current modes of
political thinking.[2] But Shakesepeare's politics cannot be defined
simply in terms of the Tudor view of history and the commonplaces of order and degree. When he inquired most deeply into
the nature of political life what incitements were offered him
to the affirmation, or reaffirmation, of positives transcending the
political?

I am not a medievalist, but even a slight acquaintance with
earlier literature suggests that the characteristics of Shakespeare's
political wisdom, which I have tried to define, had some correspondence with older forms of thinking about politics and
social life.[3] There was, for example, the medieval habit of dis-

---

[1] *Macbeth*, IV, iii, 97–100.

[2] For example, Alfred Hart's pioneering *Shakespeare and the Homilies*
(1934) and E. M. W. Tillyard's *Shakespeare's History Plays*.

[3] Professor F. P. Wilson says of Shakespeare, 'The evidence suggests that
when a theme took possession of his mind, especially a theme with a long
tradition behind it, he read widely—not laboriously, but with a darting
intelligence, which quickened his invention. . . . Somehow, like all thinking

cussing politics in terms not of masses but of men, and of men not only in one specialized aspect but in relation to all their needs, spiritual as well as material, as human beings. Thus R. W and A. J. Carlyle, writing of political theory in the thirteenth century, speak of the general conviction that 'the end and purpose of the state is a moral one—that is, the maintenance of justice, or, in the terms derived from Aristotle, the setting forward of the life according to virtue, and that the authority of the state is limited by its end—that is, by justice'.[1] Similar considerations of course lie behind the medieval formulations of economic ethics, as Professor Tawney and others have shown. This I suppose is sufficiently well known. What I should like to add is that if medieval political thought is ethical through and through, what is in question is not the legalistic application of a formula but the bringing to bear of spiritual penetration and moral insight. If Dante in the *De Monarchia* is medieval in his use—and abuse—of formal logic, he is also, I suppose, representative when he insists on the necessary connexion between love and justice:

> Just as greed, though it be never so little, clouds to some extent the disposition of justice, so does charity or right love sharpen and brighten it. . . . Greed, scorning the intrinsic significance of man, seeks other things; but charity, scorning all other things, seeks God and man, and consequently the good of man. And since, amongst the other blessings of man, living in peace is the chief . . . and justice is the chiefest and mightiest accomplisher of this, therefore

[1] R. W. Carlyle and A. J. Carlyle, *A History of Medieval Political Thought in the West*, Vol. V, *The Political Theory of the Thirteenth Century*, p. 35.

men in his day, he acquainted himself with that vast body of reflection upon the nature of man and man's place in society and in the universe which his age inherited in great part from the ancient and medieval worlds.' —'Shakespeare's Reading', in *Shakespeare Survey III* (pp. 18, 20). Professor Wilson well suggests the innumerable ways in which any one aspect of 'the tradition' might reach Shakespeare. Cf. also M. D. H. Parker, *The Slave of Life: a Study of Shakespeare and the Idea of Justice*, p. 196.

charity will chiefly give vigour to justice; and the stronger she is, the more.[1]

Similarly St Thomas Aquinas, discussing the advantages of just rule and the basic weakness of tyranny, remarks, 'there is nothing on this earth to be preferred before true friendship'; but 'fear makes a weak foundation'.[2] The significance of such comments is that although they are in the highest degree relevant and acute, they spring from an insight that is spiritual, moral, and psychological rather than political in any limited sense.

It is the same with the medieval conception of the nature and purpose of the state. For Aquinas man is by nature a social and political animal, destined therefore to live in a society which supplies his needs in far more than a merely material sense. Life in a community, he says, 'enables man to achieve a plenitude of life; not merely to exist, but to live fully, with all that is necessary to well-being'.[3] This way of thinking not only reminds us of the social character of politics, it helps to bring out the implications of the great traditional metaphor (which has behind it both Plato and the New Testament) of the body politic: the implication, above all, of co-operation and mutuality not as a vague ideal of universal benevolence but as the necessary condition, intimately felt, of individual development in its diversity. I think that John of Salisbury, in whose *Poli-*

---

[1] *De Monarchia*, Book I, Chap. 11, Temple Classics edn., p. 153. A similar passage is the opening of Book I, Chap. 13, where Dante shows 'that he who would dispose others best must himself be best disposed'—which is Duke Vincentio's

> He who the sword of heaven will bear
> Should be as holy as severe;
> Pattern in himself to know ... (*Measure for Measure*, III, ii.)

[2] Aquinas, *Selected Political Writings*, translated by J. G. Dawson, edited by A. P. d'Entrèves, pp. 55, 59. The whole passage is relevant to *Macbeth* in its political aspect.

[3] *Selected Political Writings*, p. 191. On Aquinas' conception of the State as 'the highest expression of human fellowship' see Professor d'Entrèves' Introduction, p. xv.

craticus (1159) the organic conception of the state is prominent,[1] gives life to the metaphor, reveals its sharp immediacy, when he tells how Philip of Macedon, advised to beware of a certain man, replied, 'What, if a part of my body were sick, would I cut it off rather than seek to heal it?'—or when, speaking of the prince's reluctance to administer even necessary punishment, he asks, 'Who was ever strong enough to amputate the members of his own body without grief and pain?'[2] The temptation for the modern reader is to regard the metaphor simply as a rhetorical or conventional flourish. Taken in its context it does not seem to be so, but rather to spring from a perception of the foundations of political and social life in 'the real spirit of helpfulness'.[3]

Then and then only will the health of the commonwealth be sound and flourishing when the higher members shield the lower, and the lower respond faithfully and fully in like measure to the just demands of their superiors, so that each and all are as it were members one of another by a sort of reciprocity, and each regards his own interest as best served by that which he knows to be most advantageous for the others.[4]

[1] *The Statesman's Book of John of Salisbury* (selections from the *Policraticus*), translated with an Introduction by John Dickinson (Political Science Classics Series). The editor speaks of 'the absence of any clear distinction in John's thought between the social and the political; abuse of public power is conceived simply in terms of a breach of personal morality' (p. lxvii).

[2] Op. cit., pp. 37–8. 'It was [Trajan's] habit to say that a man is insane who, having inflamed eyes, prefers to dig them out rather than cure them' (p. 39).

[3] Op. cit., p. 95.

[4] Op. cit., p. 244. In *English Literature in the Sixteenth Century* (p. 36) C. S. Lewis gives an interesting summary of an aspect of Calvin's social thought which has a similar revealing power: 'a Christian must not give "as though he would bind his brother unto him by the benefit". When I use my hands to heal some other part of my body I lay the body under no obligation to the hands: and since we are all members of one another, we similarly lay no obligation on the poor when we relieve them.'

The social and moral bias of medieval political thought also appears in the conception of the nature and duties of the ruler, who is ideally concerned not only with his own power, nor simply with the power of the state, but with the common good: 'for albeit the consul or king be masters of the rest as regards the way, yet as regards the end they are their servants'.[1]

These are random examples, I know, but it does seem that Shakespeare, in his thinking about politics, is closer to John of Salisbury than he is, say, to Hobbes: closer not only when he speaks explicitly of 'the king-becoming graces' in the great traditional terms,

> As Justice, Verity, Temp'rance, Stableness,
> Bounty, Perseverance, Mercy, Lowliness,
> Devotion, Patience, Courage, Fortitude,[2]

but also in his whole conception of a political society as a network of personal relationships, and of the health or disease of that society as ultimately dependent on the quality and nature of those relationships. If this is so, one question is how the great commonplaces of medieval political and social thinking were kept alive into the sixteenth century. By the great commonplaces I do not refer only to explicit political formulations. From the principles deriving from Greek, Roman, and Christian sources diverse political theories could be drawn; and although some of the explicit theories such as that of the ruler's responsibility to God and to his people were still alive in the sixteenth century,[3] there were also, with the changing circumstances of the age, major shifts of emphasis and direction, I refer also, and perhaps above all, to a manner of approach, and to a cast of

[1] Dante, *De Monarchia* (Temple Classics), I, 12, p. 159.
[2] *Macbeth*, IV, iii, 91 ff.
[3] On the general question of the continuity of political thought see A. P. d'Entrèves, *The Medieval Contribution to Political Thought*; J. W. Allen, *A History of Political Thought in the Sixteenth Century*, Part II, Chap. III ('A Very and True Commonweal'); and Christopher Morris, *Political Thought in England: Tyndale to Hooker*.

mind. Mr Christopher Morris says of Tudor Englishmen that they did not find it easy to think of politics except in terms of persons: they 'were still medieval enough to persist in discussing political matters in what to us are not political terms'.[1] So that our inquiry would not only take the form of an investigation into the number of times that medieval formulations reappear in political tracts and the like. It would be less concerned, for example, with the elaboration of correspondences between the individual and the state than with habits of mind implying a direct perception of mutual need, of what Hooker called 'a natural delight which man hath to transfuse from himself into others, and to receive from others into himself especially those things wherein the excellency of his kind doth most consist';[2] it would be concerned with those habits of mind without which the commonplaces remain lifeless. The great metaphors ('the body politic'), the great moral sentences ('Without justice, what are states but great bands of robbers?') not only provoke thought; for their fullest efficacy at any time they demand a habit of active apprehension. An important part of our inquiry, then, would be into the tradition of vividness and particularity in the handling of social and political questions: a tradition of which the tendency was to transform the political into the social, and the social into the religious—the tradition (shall we say?) of *Piers Plowman*.[3]

Of the habits helping to constitute the tradition something,

[1] Op. cit., pp. 1-2.
[2] *Of the Laws of Ecclesiastical Polity* (Everyman edition), I, x, 12.
[3] Of that poem it can be said, as Coleridge said of religion in *The States-man's Manual*, that it acts 'by contraction of universal truths into individual duties, as the only form in which those truths can attain life and reality'. It would be interesting to know who bought and read *Piers Plowman* in the various editions put out by Robert Crowley in 1550—'the sense', it was thought, 'somewhat dark, but not so hard, but that it may be understood of such as will not stick to break the shell of the nut for the kernel's sake'. There were three impressions in 1550; a further edition appeared in 1561. See Skeat's edition of the poem, Vol. II, pp. lxxii–lxxvi.

clearly, was due to the characteristic features of communities not yet large enough to obscure direct dealing between men with impersonal forms. But social life alone did not make the tradition: it was made by proverbs and preachings, by ballads and plays, by words read and listened to; in Elizabethan England it was largely made by the Bible.

Shakespeare's contemporary, Richard Hooker—who is also, like Shakespeare, a great representative figure—may help to direct our thoughts. In Hooker, so far as I am acquainted with him, there is not only the familiar 'medieval' insistence on the subordination of politics to ethics and religion; not only the sense that civilization, 'a life fit for the dignity of man',[1] is based on 'the good of mutual participation'[2] (and co-operation is with the dead as well as among the living): there is a disposition of mind that springs from and fosters a lively responsiveness to the actual. Hooker's sense of history, for which he is so rightly admired, is a sense of being in a concrete situation: it is allied with and encourages an unruffled acceptance of complexity,[3] and his work is a permanent antidote to the doctrinaire, simplifying mind—puritan or other. Yet the insistence on change, on the element of convention in human undertakings, is balanced by a firmness of principle that springs from an assurance of the continuity of the great affirmations. Hooker's attitude to the Bible is of interest not only to theologians and

[1] *Of the Laws of Ecclesiastical Polity* (Everyman edition), I, x, 1.

[2] 'Civil society doth more content the nature of man than any private kind of solitary living, because in society this good of mutual participation is so much larger than otherwise. Herewith notwithstanding we are not satisfied, but we covet (if it might be) to have a kind of society and fellowship even with all mankind' (I, x, 12).

[3] 'The bounds of wisdom are large, and within them much is contained.... We may not so in any one special kind admire her, that we disgrace her in any other; but let all her ways be according unto their place and degree adored' (II, i, 4). As Hooker says elsewhere, 'Carry peaceable minds and ye may have comfort by this variety', 'A Learned Discourse of Justification', op. cit., Vol. I, p. 75.

students of church history. Completely free from what Professor d'Entrèves calls 'the narrow and intolerant scripturalism of the puritans',[1] Hooker's appeal to the Bible is that of a free and reasonable mind for which the Bible has a special authority. And the relevance of this fact to our inquiry into the more-than-political tradition becomes clear when we recall *The Statesman's Manual* of Coleridge. The Bible, he said, was 'the best guide to political skill and foresight' because its events and prescriptions demand a response of the whole man, because they embody universal principles in the sharply particular. 'In nothing', he said, 'is Scriptural history more strongly contrasted with the histories of highest note in the present age, than in its freedom from the hollowness of abstractions': its symbolic actuality ('incorporating the reason in images of the sense') offers the strongest possible contrast to histories and political theories produced by the 'unenlivened generalizing understanding'.[2] Remembering this, we may perhaps understand why 'the strange immediacy of scriptural history'[3] in the age of Shakespeare had a very decided bearing on the way in which the best minds sought to understand political situations.

What bearing this, and the other matters I have touched on, had on the practice of the age would be a separate study. When we think in turn of the adult political wisdom of Shakespeare and the tradition informing that wisdom, then of certain aspects of Elizabethan-Jacobean political life, its greed, faction and unscrupulousness,[4] inevitably a question confronts us. A

[1] *The Medieval Contribution to Political Thought*, p. 104.
[2] See *The Statesman's Manual*, in *Political Tracts of Wordsworth, Coleridge and Shelley*, ed. R. J. White, pp. 18, 24, 28 and *passim*. Mr White's Introduction gives a valuable account of this aspect of Coleridge's thought.
[3] David Mathew, *The Jacobean Age*, p. 14. 'The biblical characters were very close and they overshadowed the chronicles and the heraldry' (p. 15).
[4] See, for example, the closing pages of Professor J. E. Neale's Raleigh Lecture for 1948, 'The Elizabethan Political Scene', *Proc. Brit. Acad.*, vol. xxxiv.

cynical answer would be out of place. The passion of Dante does not prove that he came from a just city: rather, as we know, the reverse. Yet how much it meant that Italy in the thirteenth century, even in the conditions we know, should produce a Dante! Mr T. S. Eliot, borrowing the term from Canon Demant, speaks of 'the *pre-political* area', where the imaginative writer exercises his true political function. 'And my defence of the importance of the *pre-political*', he says, 'is simply this, that it is the stratum down to which any sound political thinking must push its roots, and from which it must derive its nourishment.'[1] That in the imperfect conditions of Elizabethan-Jacobean England something was kept alive in the pre-political area that was of the greatest importance for the health of a political society, Shakespeare's plays (and not these alone) are the living witness. When we try to define what it was that was kept alive we find ourselves with a renewed sense of the meaning and nature of a tradition whose significance for us today should need no arguing. Towards the end of the Third Satire Donne says,

> That thou mayest rightly obey power, her bounds know;
> Those past, her nature, and name is chang'd; to be
> Then humble to her is idolatry.

Shakespeare's political plays are creative explorations of conceptions such as power, authority, honour, order, and freedom, which only too easily become objects of 'idolatry'. Their real meaning is only revealed when political life is seen, as Shakespeare makes us see it, in terms of the realities of human life and human relationships. As Aristotle said long ago, 'Clearly the student of politics must know somehow the facts about soul.'[2]

[1] *The Literature of Politics* (Conservative Political Centre), p. 22.
[2] *Ethics* (translated by W. D. Ross), I, xiii.

Personality and Politics in
Julius Caesar

SHAKESPEARE wrote *Julius Caesar* in 1599, and the play was first performed in the new theatre, the Globe, which Shakespeare's company, the Lord Chamberlain's Men, had recently had built on the Bankside. Shakespeare, of course, got the material for his play from Plutarch's *Lives* of Caesar and Brutus. But, just as in gathering material for the English historical plays from Holinshed, he selected only what he needed as an artist dealing with the universal stuff of human nature, so here his purpose is not simply to reconstruct the historical situation in Rome in the year 44 B.C. The historical material is of interest only for what Shakespeare makes of it. That he made of it a pretty exciting drama is witnessed by the fact that the play is still being performed today, still capable of holding audiences not all of whom are compelled by the exigencies of university examinations. It is exciting; it is richly human; it holds the attention. It also happens to be an important work of art—which means that through the forms of a dramatic action it focuses a particular vision of life: the sequence of events, the dialogue, the interplay of different characters, are held together by an informing 'idea', so that all these elements contribute not solely to an evening's entertainment but to an imaginative statement about something of permanent importance in human life. What, at that level of understanding, is *Julius Caesar* 'about'? That is the question to which I want to attempt an answer.

Before tackling that question directly, there are two matters I want to touch on—one concerning the play's structure, the other its substance: they are, in fact, closely related. The action of *Julius Caesar* turns on a political murder, the assassination of

33

Caesar, which takes place in Act III, scene i—right in the middle of the play. Before the murder, attention is focused on the origin and development of the conspiracy—Caesar on one side, Cassius, Brutus, and half a dozen more, on the other. After the murder, attention is focused on the struggle between the conspirators (Brutus and Cassius) and the successors of Caesar (Octavius Caesar and Antony), on the failure and disintegration of the republican cause. It is possible to see a blemish here: the climax, it can be said, comes too early, and when Caesar has disappeared from the action, Shakespeare only contrives to hold our interest by such *tours de force* as Antony's oration and the quarrel between Brutus and Cassius. In fact, however, the play forms a coherent and tightly woven whole. The murder of Caesar is, if you like, the axis on which the world of the play turns. Up to that event, we are shown one half of that world, a hemisphere; as soon as the daggers are plunged into Caesar's body the world of the drama turns, and fresh scenes and landscapes come into view: but it is still one world. Dropping the metaphor, we may say that the interests aroused in the first part find their natural fulfilment in the second: that there is nothing in the presented action of the last two and a half acts (and action includes psychological as well as physical action) that is not a revelation of what was implicit, but partly concealed, in the conspiracy itself. There is no question here of a broken-backed play in which flagging interest must be maintained by adventitious means. The play is as much of a unity as *Macbeth*; and, like *Macbeth*, though less powerfully, it reveals the connexion between observable events in the public world and their causes in the deeper places of personal life—matters not so easily observed except by the eye of the poet.

My second preliminary observation concerns the nature of the interest enlisted by this play. In dealing with *Julius Caesar*, as indeed with other of Shakespeare's plays, there is a particular temptation to be guarded against—that is, the temptation to abstract from the play certain general issues and to debate them either in the abstract or in a context which Shakespeare has not provided for them. Criticism of *Julius Caesar* is sometimes confused by considerations that apply either to the historical situation at Rome at the time of Caesar's assassination, or else to specifically twentieth-century political situations, and the play is debated as though Shakespeare were putting before us the question of whether dictatorship or republicanism were the more desirable form of government. He is doing nothing of the kind; and perhaps the first thing to notice is how much of possible political interest the play leaves out. There is no hint of, say, Dante's conception of the majesty, the providential necessity, of the empire which Caesar founded. On the other hand, there is nothing that can be interpreted as a feeling for the virtues of aristocratic republicanism—in the way, for example, some of the first makers of the French Revolution felt when they invoked Roman example. We are not called on to concern ourselves with whether 'Caesarism' is, or was, desirable or otherwise. Instead, there is a sharp focus on a single, simple, but important question—on what happens when personal judgment tries to move exclusively on a political plane, where issues are simplified and distorted. I may say, in passing, that if we want a wider context for the play, we shall find it not in a realm of political speculation foreign to it, but in those other plays of Shakespeare—they include such different plays as *Troilus and Cressida* and *Othello*—where the dramatist is posing the question of how men come to deliver themselves to illusion, of how they construct for themselves a world in which, because it is not the world of reality but a projection of their own, they inevitably come to disaster. This means, of course, that the play offers no solution—it offers no material for a solution—of the question, Empire or Republic? dictatorship or 'liberty'? Shakespeare is studying a situation, bringing the force of his imagination to bear on it, not offering solutions, or not, at all events, political ones.

Yet—and this brings me to the substance of what I want to say—*Julius Caesar* does have important political implications. It takes up Shakespeare's developing preoccupation with the relation between political action and morality. 'Politics', I know, is an exciting word, and 'morality' is a dry word. But what I mean is this:—Politics are the realm where, whatever the particular interests involved, the issues are to some extent simplified and generalized, and therefore seen in abstract and schematic terms. Morality—and I mean essential living morality, not just copy-book maxims—has to do with the human, the specific and particular. Martin Buber, in his great book, *I and Thou*, has made us familiar with an important distinction —between the world of 'thou' (the world of relationship) and the world of 'it' (the world where things, and even people, are treated simply as objects, and manipulated accordingly). For the politician there is a constant temptation to lose sight of the 'thou' world, and Martin Buber's distinction may help us here.

Julius Caesar is a play about great public events, but again and again we are given glimpses of the characters in their private, personal, and domestic capacities. Caesar is concerned for his wife's barrenness, he faints when he is offered the crown, he 'had a sickness when he was in Spain', he listens to Calpurnia's dreams and fears. Brutus causes his wife concern about his health; we are told of his disturbed sleep; we see him forgetting his public cares and ensuring, with real tenderness, that his boy Lucius gets some needed sleep. And much more to a similar effect. Now Shakespeare at this time was nearing the height of his powers—*Hamlet* is only a year or two away—and it is unlikely that he put in these domestic scenes and glimpses because he didn't know what else to do. It is obvious that we are intended to be aware of some sort of a *contrast* between public life and private, and commentators have, in fact, noticed

this. They point, for example, to the contrast between Caesar
the public figure and Caesar the man:

> . . . for always I am Caesar.
> Come on my right hand, for this ear is deaf.

When Brutus, in his 'gown' (the symbol of domestic privacy)
speaks gently to his boy, we are told that this 'relieves the
strain' of the tragic action. And every account of the characters
includes some reference to those aspects of Caesar, Brutus, and
Cassius that are revealed in their more intimate moments and
hidden or disguised in public. What seems not to have been
recognized is the cumulative effect of these and many other
reminders of a more personal life—the important part this
pervasive but unobtrusive personalism plays, or should play, in
our evaluation of the public action.

That we are intended to be aware of the characters as men,
of the faces behind the masks, is clear enough. We may notice
in passing that on occasion the contrast is emphasized in visual
terms. At the beginning of II, ii, according to the stage-
direction that makes every schoolboy laugh, Caesar enters 'in
his night-gown' (a dressing-gown, or house-coat); then, as the
conspirators prevail over his wife's entreaties, 'Give me my
robe, for I will go.' Not only are all the main figures at some
time divested of their public robes—those 'robes and furr'd
gowns' that, according to King Lear, 'hide all'—and allowed to
appear as husbands, masters of households and friends, but they
all, in turn, emphasize each other's personal characteristics. 'He
was quick mettle when he went to school,' says Brutus of
Casca. A principal reason why Cassius thinks Caesar isn't fit
for his exalted position is that he, Cassius, is the stronger
swimmer, and that Caesar, like the rest of us, was hot and cold
and thirsty when he had a fever. And although Antony, addressing the crowd, deliberately makes emotional capital out of
Caesar's mantle, 'I remember,' he says,

> The first time Caesar ever put it on;
> 'Twas on a summer's evening, in his tent,
> That day he overcame the Nervii,

the touch of particularity, of revealed privacy, is intended for us, the audience, as well as for the Roman crowd. We notice, too, how often the word 'love' appears in this play. I haven't made a count, but it must be about two dozen times, which is perhaps rather surprising in a political play. Again and again the characters speak of their love—their 'dear love' or their 'kind love'—for each other, just as they seem to find a special satisfaction in referring to themselves as 'brothers'. Now the effect of all this is not only one of pathos or simple irony. The focus of our attention, I have said, is the public world: from the arena of *that* world, personal life—where truth between man and man resides—is glimpsed as across a gulf. The distance between these two worlds is the measure of the distortion and falsity that takes place in the attempt to make 'politics' self-enclosed.

The attempt—the attempt to make public action and public appearance something separate and remote from personal action—is common to both sides. Caesar constantly assumes the public mask. It seems to be a habit with him to refer to himself in the third person as 'Caesar'; and there is his speech, so charged with dramatic irony, when, immediately before the assassination, he rejects the petition of Metellus Cimber:

> I could be well mov'd if I were as you;
> If I could pray to move, prayers would move me;
> But I am constant as the northern star,
> Of whose true-fix'd and resting quality
> There is no fellow in the firmament . . .
> So in the world; 'tis furnish'd well with men,
> And men are flesh and blood, and apprehensive;
> Yet in the number I do know but one
> That unassailable holds on his rank,

> Unshak'd of motion: and that I am he,
> Let me a little show it. . . .

What this means, in the case of Caesar, is that in the utterance and attitude of the public man we sense a dangerous tautness. In the case of Brutus, a parallel divorce between the man and the statesman results in something more subtle and more interesting. That a particular bond of affection unites Caesar and Brutus, the play leaves us in no doubt. Almost the first words that Brutus speaks of Caesar are, 'I love him well', and when, after the murder, he insists again and again that Caesar was his 'best lover', there is no need to doubt his 'sincerity' in the ordinary sense of the word. So, too, Cassius tells us, 'Caesar doth bear me hard; but he loves Brutus'; and Mark Antony:

> For Brutus, as you know, was Caesar's angel:
> Judge, O you Gods! how dearly Caesar lov'd him.
> This was the most unkindest cut of all. . . .

It is this Brutus, the close friend of Caesar, who wrenches his mind to divorce policy from friendship; and the way in which he does it demands some attention.

It is, of course, true that on matters of public policy you may have to take a firm stand against men whom on other grounds you like and respect: you can see this in the government of a university, for example, as well as in the government of a state. Is Brutus doing more than follow this principle to a necessary conclusion? Well, yes, I think he is. For the moment I want to put on one side the scene in which Cassius (in Brutus's own words later) 'whets' him against Caesar, and ask your attention for the long soliloquy at the opening of Act II in which Brutus reviews his own motives and intended course of action. This is what he says:

> It must be by his death: and for my part,
> I know no personal cause to spurn at him,
> But for the general. He would be crown'd:

39

How that might change his nature, there's the question.
It is the bright day that brings forth the adder;
And that craves wary walking. Crown him! that!
And then, I grant, we put a sting in him,
That at his will he may do danger with.
The abuse of greatness is when it disjoins
Remorse from power; and, to speak truth of Caesar,
I have not known when his affections sway'd
More than his reason. But 'tis a common proof,
That lowliness is young ambition's ladder,
Whereto the climber-upward turns his face;
And when he once attains the upmost round,
He then unto the ladder turns his back,
Looks in the clouds, scorning the base degrees
By which he did ascend. So Caesar may:
Then, lest he may, prevent. And, since the quarrel
Will bear no colour for the thing he is,
Fashion it thus; that what he is, augmented,
Would run to these and these extremities;
And therefore think him as a serpent's egg
Which, hatch'd, would, as his kind, grow mischievous,
And kill him in the shell.

Now it is a principle of Shakespearean, indeed of Elizabethan, stage-craft, that when a character, in soliloquy or otherwise, develops a line of argument—as when Faustus, in Marlowe's play, produces a number of specious reasons for dismissing the traditional sciences—we are expected to follow the argument with some attention. Not, of course, that we follow such a speech merely as logicians. We are dealing with drama, which means that when a character expounds, say, his reasons for a course of action, what he says is intended to reveal some aspect of what he stands for and is committed to as a human being. And we are dealing with *poetic* drama, which means that even in an expository speech we are aware of much more than can be formulated in conceptual terms. But we do not, on this account, switch off our intelligence or such powers of logical thought as we may possess. As Virgil Whitaker says in his book, *Shakespeare's Use of Learning*, 'Like Marlowe, Shakespeare expected his audience to be able to detect a fallacy in reasoning.' With this in mind, let us turn back to Brutus's soliloquy. It is a curious argument, in which qualities known in direct contact between man and man ('I know no personal cause to spurn at him') are dismissed as irrelevant to public considerations; and it is precisely this that gives the air of tortuous unreality to Brutus's self-persuadings—full as these are of subjunctives and conditional verbs, which run full tilt against the reality that Brutus himself acknowledges:

> The abuse of greatness is when it disjoins
> Remorse from power; and, to speak truth of Caesar,
> I have not known when his affections sway'd
> More than his reason. . . .[1]

but:

> since the quarrel
> Will bear no colour for the thing he is,
> Fashion it thus. . . .

On this Coleridge shrewdly commented that what Brutus is really saying is that he 'would have no objection to a king, or to Caesar as a monarch in Rome, would Caesar but be as good a monarch as he now seems disposed to be'. In Brutus's mind, however, *what is* is now completely lost in a cloud of mere possibilities:

> And since the quarrel
> Will bear no colour for the thing he is,
> Fashion it thus; that what he is, augmented,
> Would run to these and these extremities;
> And therefore think him as a serpent's egg
> Which, hatch'd, would, as his kind, grow mischievous,
> And kill him in the shell.

[1] It may not be unnecessary to comment that 'remorse', here, means pity, and 'affections', passions.

Caesar is already, as Brutus describes him later, 'the foremost man of all the world'; he is not still 'in the shell', neither is he 'young ambition'. But it is by sophistries such as these that Brutus launches himself on what Clarendon was to call 'that fathomless abyss of Reason of State'.

Shakespeare, of course, was a very great psychologist, and what the play also shows—and I want to dwell on this for a moment before returning to the scene of Brutus's crucial choice and its consequences—is that personal feelings, which Brutus tries to exclude from his deliberations on 'the general good', are, in fact, active in public life. But they are active in the wrong way. Unacknowledged, they influence simply by distorting the issues. The famous quarrel scene between Brutus and Cassius certainly has this ironic significance. It is, of course, Cassius, in whom the 'taboo on tenderness' is strongest—who is scornful of 'our mothers' spirits' (I, iii, 83) and despises Caesar for behaving 'as a sick girl' (I, ii, 127)—who here displays the most pronounced 'feminine' traits—'that rash humour which my mother gave me' (IV, iii, 119). That the whole thing contrives to be touching should not obscure the fact that the causes of the quarrel—they had mainly to do with money—did demand a more impersonal consideration. Now the relevance of this is that it is above all in Cassius that the springs of political action are revealed as only too personal. What nags at him is simply envy of Caesar: 'for my single self', he says to Brutus:

> I had as lief not be as live to be
> In awe of such a thing as I myself. . . .
> . . . And this man
> Is now become a god, and Cassius is
> A wretched creature and must bend his body
> If Caesar carelessly but nod on him.

Caesar, he says to Casca, is:

> A man no mightier than thyself or me
> In personal action, yet prodigious grown.

And it is this man who acts as tempter to the 'idealizing' Brutus, skilfully enlisting what Brutus feels is due to his own 'honour'. I do not wish here to pursue the temptation scene in any detail; but that it *is* temptation the play leaves us in no doubt. At the end of the long, skilfully conducted second scene of the first act, Cassius is left alone and reveals his thoughts about the man whom we can only call, at this stage, his dupe:

> Well, Brutus, thou art noble; yet, I see,
> Thy honourable mettle may be wrought
> From that it is dispos'd; therefore 'tis meet
> That noble minds keep ever with their likes;
> For who so firm that cannot be seduc'd?

Editors disagree about the meaning of these lines. Some would have it that Cassius means that the noble disposition of Brutus may be, as it were, wrenched from truth by his friendship with Caesar, the dictator: the man of republican virtue should 'keep ever' with those like-minded to himself. It may be so; but I find it hard *not* to read the lines as a firm 'placing' comment on Cassius's own relations with Brutus: 'For who so firm that cannot be seduc'd'—by specious reasoning? The most we can say for Cassius is that his appeals to Roman 'honour', to the 'nobility' of his associates, are not simply laid on for the benefit of Brutus, but are part of his own self-deception. The banished feelings have come in by the back door, thinly disguised by much talk of 'honour'.

It is of course true that the play does not present Caesar as an ideal ruler, and I myself think that Shakespeare would have agreed with Blake's gnomic verse:

> The strongest poison ever known
> Came from Caesar's laurel crown.

But when Brutus, the man of honour and high moral principles, accepts Cassius's arguments and enters the world of the conspirators, he enters a topsyturvy world—a world where 'impersonal' Reasons of State take the place of direct personal knowledge; and at the same time true reason, which is a function of the whole man, has given way to obscure personal emotion. Shakespeare leaves us in no doubt of the confusion of values and priorities in that world. We have noticed how often love and friendship are invoked in this play, indicating what men really want and need. What we also have to notice is how often the forms of friendship are exploited for political ends. When Caesar is reluctant to go to the Senate House, Decius inveigles him with protestations of 'dear dear love', and the conspirators drink wine with their victim before leading him to the Capitol; Brutus kisses Caesar immediately before the killing; Antony talks much of love and shakes hands all round as a way of deceiving the conspirators. It is this, therefore, that explains our sense of something monstrous in the action, symbolized by the storms and prodigies, and made fully explicit by Brutus in his garden soliloquy—for it is time to return to that—when, deserting the actual, he has given himself to a phantasmagoria of abstractions.

At this point, Brutus's self-communings are interrupted by his boy, Lucius, who brings him a letter—one of many such, purporting to come from the citizens of Rome asking for redress at his hands, but, as we know, manufactured by Cassius. 'O Rome!' says Brutus, not knowing that the letters do not represent 'Rome' at all,

> O Rome! I make thee promise;
> If the redress will follow, thou receiv'st
> Thy full petition at the hand of Brutus!

Then, as Lucius goes off once more to see who is knocking at the gate in the darkness:

> Since Cassius first did whet me against Caesar,
> I have not slept.
> Between the acting of a dreadful thing

> And the first motion, all the interim is
> Like a phantasma, or a hideous dream:
> The genius and the mortal instruments
> Are then in council; and the state of man,
> Like to a little kingdom, suffers then
> The nature of an insurrection.

The indications here—the insomnia, the fact that Brutus is, as he has said earlier, 'with himself at war'—are, if we remember *Macbeth*, clear enough. And the signs of a mind at war with itself, attempting to batten down its own best insights, which yet refuse to disappear, continue into Brutus's musings as the muffled conspirators are announced:

> O conspiracy!
> Sham'st thou to show thy dangerous brow by night,
> When evils are most free? O! then by day
> Where wilt thou find a cavern dark enough
> To mask thy monstrous visage? Seek none, conspiracy;
> Hide it in smiles and affability:
> For if thou path, thy native semblance on,
> Not Erebus itself were dim enough
> To hide thee from prevention.

Conspiracy is not only 'dangerous', it is 'monstrous', associated with night and darkness, with evils and Erebus. As J. I. M. Stewart has said, Brutus's words are those of a 'man over the threshold of whose awareness a terrible doubt perpetually threatens to lap'.

Brutus, of course, is not a deliberate villain as Macbeth is; but like Macbeth he is presented as losing his way in a nightmare world—'like a phantasma', something both horrible and unreal, 'or a hideous dream'. In other words, Brutus's wrong choice not only leads to wrong action, it delivers him to a world of unreality, for the 'phantasma', far from ending with the acting of the 'dreadful thing', extends beyond it. As the play proceeds, we are made aware not only of a complete lack of correspondence between the professed intentions of the conspirators and the result of their act, but of a marked element of unreality in the world which they inhabit. Let us take two examples, for Shakespeare provides them, and he presumably intended that we should take notice of what he provides.

Shakespeare often puts before the audience two different aspects of the same thing, or suggests two different angles on it —sometimes, but not always, in juxtaposed scenes. He makes no obvious comment, but the different scenes or passages play off against each other, with an effect of implicit comment, for the audience itself is thus enlisted in the business of evaluation and judgment. I think of such things as Falstaff's description of his ragged regiment, following hard on the heels of Hotspur's heroics about warfare, in the First Part of *Henry IV*; or the way in which, in *Antony and Cleopatra* the summit meeting on Pompey's galley is followed immediately by a glimpse of the army in the field, with some irony from a soldier about the High Command. In *Julius Caesar*, the murder of Caesar is not only presented on the stage, it is described both in prospect and in retrospect. You all remember the way in which Brutus envisages the action to the conspirators in the scene with which we have been dealing. Pleading that Antony may be spared, he says:

> Let us be sacrificers, but not butchers, Caius.
> We all stand up against the spirit of Caesar;
> And in the spirit of men there is no blood:
> O! that we then could come by Caesar's spirit,
> And not dismember Caesar. But, alas!
> Caesar must bleed for it. And, gentle friends,
> Let's kill him boldly, but not wrathfully;
> Let's carve him as a dish fit for the gods,
> Not hew him as a carcass fit for hounds. . . .

Is that the way political assassinations are carried out? Before

46

the battle of Philippi, Brutus taunts Antony, 'you very wisely
threat before you sting', to which Antony retorts:

> Villains! you did not so when your vile daggers
> Hack'd one another in the sides of Caesar;
> You show'd your teeth like apes, and fawn'd like hounds,
> And bow'd like bondmen, kissing Caesar's feet;
> Whilst damned Casca, like a cur, behind,
> Struck Caesar on the neck.

Antony, of course, speaks as a partisan of Caesar, but the energy
of the verse ('your vile daggers Hack'd one another in the sides
of Caesar') leaves us in no doubt that Antony's account is
nearer to actuality than Brutus's fantasy of a ritualistic sacrifice.

My second example is of even greater importance, for it
concerns the whole sequence of events in the second half of the
play—consequences, I want to insist once more, that are shown
as flowing directly from what Brutus and the rest commit
themselves to in the first part. As soon as Julius Caesar falls,
Cinna cries out:

> Liberty! Freedom! Tyranny is dead!
> Run hence, proclaim, cry it about the streets.

And Cassius:

> Some to the common pulpits, and cry out
> 'Liberty, freedom, and enfranchisement!'

Then, as something of the mounting bewilderment outside the
Capitol is conveyed to us ('Men, wives, and children stare, cry
out and run As it were doomsday'), Brutus enforces the ritualistic action of smearing themselves with Caesar's blood:

> Stoop, Romans, stoop,
> And let us bathe our hands in Caesar's blood
> Up to the elbows, and besmear our swords:
> Then walk we forth, even to the market-place;
> And, waving our red weapons o'er our heads,
> Let's all cry, 'Peace, freedom, and liberty!'

The irony of that hardly needs comment, but the play does, in fact, comment on it with some pungency. I suspect that what I am going to say will be obvious, so I will be brief and do little more than remind you of three successive scenes. When, after the murder, Brutus goes to the Forum to render 'public reasons' for Caesar's death, it is his failure in the sense of reality, of what people really are, that gives us the sombre comedy of his oration: so far as addressing real people is concerned he might as well have kept quiet. 'Had you rather Caesar were living, and die all slaves, than that Caesar were dead, to live all free men?' he asks, and much more to the same effect. To which the reply is successively:

—Live, Brutus! live! live!
—Bring him with triumph home unto his house.
—Give him a statue with his ancestors.
—Let him be Caesar.

After this, the response of the crowd to Antony's more consummate demonstration of the arts of persuasion comes as no surprise: it is:

Revenge!—About!—Seek!—Burn!—Fire!—Kill!
—Slay!—Let not a traitor live!

Mischief, in the words of Antony's cynical comment when he has worked his will with the crowd, is indeed afoot; and the very next scene—the last of the third Act—gives us a representative example of what is only too likely to happen in times of violent political disturbance. It shows us the death of an unoffending poet at the hands of a brutal mob:

—Your name, sir, truly.
—Truly, my name is Cinna.
—Tear him to pieces; he's a conspirator.
—I am Cinna the poet, I am Cinna the poet.
—Tear him for his bad verses, tear him for his bad verses.

The frenzied violence of this, with its repeated, 'Tear him, tear him!' is followed at once by a scene of violence in a different

48

key. If the mob is beyond the reach of reason, the Triumvirs, Antony, Octavius, and Lepidus, are only too coldly calculating in their assessment of political exigencies:

> *Ant.* These many then shall die; their names are prick'd.
> *Oct.* Your brother too must die; consent you, Lepidus?
> *Lep.* I do consent—
> *Oct.*   Prick him down. Antony.
> *Lep.* Upon condition Publius shall not live,
> Who is your sister's son, Mark Antony.
> *Ant.* He shall not live; look, with a spot I damn him.
> But, Lepidus, go you to Caesar's house;
> Fetch the will hither, and we shall determine
> How to cut off some charge in legacies.

And, when Lepidus goes off on his errand, Antony and Octavius discuss the matter of getting rid of him, before they turn their attention to combating the armies now levied by Brutus and Cassius. These, then, are the more or less explicit comments on Brutus's excited proclamation:

> And, waving our red weapons o'er our heads,
> Let's all cry, 'Peace, freedom, and liberty!'

That peace and liberty could be bought with 'red weapons' was the illusion: the reality is mob violence, proscription, and civil war.

In following the story through to its end, Shakespeare was, of course, bound to follow his historical material; but, as an artist, he made this serve his own purposes. Many of you must have noticed how often Shakespeare, in his greater plays, makes the outward action into a mirror or symbol of events and qualities in the mind or soul: *Macbeth* is perhaps the most obvious instance of this. The last act of *Julius Caesar* certainly follows this pattern. Even before the battle of Philippi Brutus and Cassius appear like men under a doom; and, although defeat comes to each in different ways, it comes to both as though they were expecting it, and prompts reflections, in themselves or in their followers, that clearly apply not merely to the immediate events but to the action as a whole. Cassius asks Pindarus to report to him what is happening in another part of the field ('My sight was ever thick,' he says), and, on a mistaken report that his messenger is taken by the enemy, kills himself. On which the comment of Messala is:

> O hateful error, melancholy's child!
> Why dost thou show to the apt thoughts of men
> The things that are not? O error! soon conceiv'd,
> Thou never com'st unto a happy birth,
> But kill'st the mother that engender'd thee.

Harold Goddard, in his interesting chapter on *Julius Caesar*, says of this, 'The whole plot against Caesar had been such an error.'[1] We may add further that the play also enforces the close connexion between error and a supposed perception of 'things that are not'. As Titinius says to the dead Cassius a moment later, 'Alas! thou hast misconstrued everything.' As for Brutus, defeated and brought to bay with his 'poor remains of friends', he senses that this is no accident of defeat but the working out of the destiny to which he committed himself long before:

> Night hangs upon mine eyes; my bones would rest,
> That have but labour'd to attain this hour.

And then, as he runs on his own sword:

> Caesar, now be still:
> I kill'd not thee with half so good a will.

These last ten words—if I may quote Goddard once more— 'are the Last Judgment of Brutus on a conspiracy the morality of which other men, strangely, have long debated'.[2] Earlier in the play, you may remember, Cicero had commented on certain portents and men's interpretation of them:

[1] Harold Goddard, *The Meaning of Shakespeare*, Vol. I, p. 329.
[2] Ibid.

> But men may construe things after their fashion,
> Clean from the purpose of the things themselves.

That seems to me an anticipatory summing-up of Brutus's whole political career, as the play presents it.

Let me repeat once more, Brutus was not, in any of the ordinary senses of the word, a villain; he was simply an upright man who made a tragic mistake. The nature of that mistake the play, I think, sufficiently demonstrates. Brutus was a man who thought that an abstract 'common good' could be achieved without due regard to the complexities of the actual; a man who tried to divorce his political thinking and his political action from what he knew, and what he was, as a full human person. Many of us remember the idealizing sympathy felt by liberal young men in the 1930s for the Communist cause. There had, it was felt, been excesses, but as against the slow cruelty of a ruthless competitive society, its degradation of human values, even violence might seem like surgery. 'Today,' said W. H. Auden, in his poem, 'Spain' (1937):

> Today the inevitable increase in the chances of death;
> The conscious acceptance of guilt in the necessary murder.

That, of course, was written before the Russian treason trials of 1938 and the subsequent purges, and Auden subsequently re-wrote the lines; but they serve to illustrate the matter in hand. 'General good,' said Blake, 'is the cry of the scoundrel and the hypocrite; he who would do good to another must do it in minute particulars.' There is some exaggeration in the first half of that aphorism, but it contains a profound truth, sufficiently demonstrated in many eminent figures in history. Shakespeare demonstrates it in the figure of a man who was neither a scoundrel nor a hypocrite:

> This was the noblest Roman of them all:
> All the conspirators save only he

Did that they did in envy of great Caesar;
He only, in a general honest thought
And common good to all, made one of them.
His life was gentle, and the elements
So mix'd in him that Nature might stand up
And say to all the world, 'This was a man!'

Shakespeare offers little comfort to those who like to consider historical conflicts in terms of a simple black and white, or who imagine that there are simple solutions for political dilemmas. In the contrast between the 'gentle' Brutus and the man who, for abstract reasons ('a general honest thought'), murdered his friend and let loose civil war, Shakespeare gives us food for thought that, firmly anchored in a particular action, has a special relevance for us today, as I suspect it will have at all times.

Poetry, Politics, and the English Tradition

AN inaugural lecture can be a very grand affair, a public stocktaking in which a master of his subject defines its scope, purpose, and methods, both in relation to the general field of knowledge and as a university discipline. Or it can be something much less ambitious, an occasion when a representative of a particular branch of learning produces a sample of his wares that he thinks may be of some interest to representatives of other branches. I have chosen to produce a sample rather than to take stock. My subject-matter is indicated in a general way by the title of my lecture which might have been more aptly called 'Some Reflections prompted by Shakespeare's Handling of Political Themes'. But I have not entirely resisted the temptation offered by the opportunity of explaining to those who profess other subjects why there is nothing quite like my own. It is with a brief consideration of the nature and value of English studies in the University that I wish to begin.

In the last quarter of a century the teaching of English in universities has undergone considerable change. We do, I think, see more clearly now than was seen thirty years ago that at the centre of any literary study is the act of individual apprehension of meanings; that our first job as teachers of English is to help our students to cultivate the habit of disciplined attention to words through which the values of literature are revealed: there is no other way in which they can possess—really possess —the material of their study. Other disciplines—linguistic, textual, historical—are also properly cultivated by those who profess English in a university but they are ancillary to that central purpose of an English school, that each mind shall make

53

its own direct, personal, and unique response to the literature of the present and the past.

But this is not all. Literary studies can never remain exclusively 'literary'. *The Advancement of Learning, The Character of a Trimmer, Culture and Anarchy* (to take some random examples) —these are not works of imaginative literature but they are proper objects of study in an English school: at all events it would be an odd English School that excluded such works from its view. And if we study them at all, unless we study them merely—dreadful thought!—as 'examples of prose style', we are bound to consider their subject-matter, whether it is the philosophy of progress, politics, or the question of culture. As for works of imaginative literature—*King Lear, The Canterbury Tales* or *Middlemarch*—we are interested in them because they all in different ways focus what Arnold called 'the great question,—How to Live?'—they spring from a passionate interest in the general life and lead back to it. Since English is still comparatively a newcomer in our universities it may help to make my point if I invoke one of the great established disciplines. I do not know Greek, but it seems safe to say that the great educational value of Greek is this: that it involves the study of a literature that includes not only great poetry of many kinds but philosophy, ethics, history, and political theory, together with the study of the social experience—the living body of language, traditions, and institutions—out of which these sprang; that it forces the student to consider deeply, under the guidance of great masters and in a particular historical setting, some of the central problems of human existence, whilst bringing him back again and again to take active possession of masterpieces whose essential existence transcends the temporal and is in the living here and now.

It is a similar claim that I should make for English studies. As compared with Classical Greek, English Literature presents the difficulty that it is still going on. Indeed I am tempted to say that the only disadvantage of English is that there is so much of it: from Yeats and Eliot back to *Beowulf* one stumbles as best one can. But it has the great advantage that its material—that which prompts the student to fresh thought, fresh perception and the imaginative apprehension of life—is the language that he habitually uses for thought and expression; a language that, because it is an intimate part of his own life as lived, has a depth and resonance he can hardly hope to feel in a language not his own, and that comes home to him therefore with unsurpassable vividness and force.

My position then is this. The student of English is in the first place a student of literature, of works great and small in which something of permanent interest and value is embodied. But he is also—I think necessarily—a student of a way of life, changing with the years but with a recognizable continuity and tradition, and at all times capable of shedding light on questions that will confront him not simply as a university student, not simply as a student of literature in any restricted sense, but as a man living the common life of men. My lecture is an attempt to illustrate, by means of a particular example, how the study of literature can properly lead beyond literature, to fields of interest common to all who, whether within universities or without, reflect on life at all.

1

My starting-point is Shakespeare's characteristic handling of political themes. Shakespeare, of course, was not a political writer in the sense in which Milton and Dryden were sometimes political writers: he had no cause to support, and it is unwise to extract from his plays a set of 'views' on political questions and attribute them to him. But he was deeply interested in the nature of kingship and authority, in statecraft and in men's relations with each other in the sphere of public life; and if there is no Shakespearean political doctrine there is a recognizably Shakespearean manner in the dramatic presentation of political situations and problems. It is a manner suggested by a few lines in the scenes attributed to Shakespeare in the play, *Sir Thomas More*. At this point in the play there is a riot of apprentices because of the presence in London of foreign workmen, and More, as Sheriff, addresses the rioters:

> Grant them removed, and grant that this your noise
> Hath chid down all the majesty of England;
> Imagine that you see the wretched strangers,
> Their babies at their backs, with their poor luggage,
> Plodding to the ports and coasts for transportation,
> And that you sit as kings in your desires,
> Authority quite silenced by your brawl
> And you in ruff of your opinions clothed,—
> What had you got? I'll tell you, you had taught
> How insolence and strong hand should prevail,
> How order should be quelled, and by this pattern
> Not one of you should live an aged man.
> For other ruffians as their fancies wrought,
> With self same hand self reasons and self right,
> Would shark on you, and men like ravenous fishes
> Would feed on one another.

The speech is interesting because it shows the preoccupation with public order that is sometimes regarded—too simply perhaps—as all we really know of Shakespeare's political philosophy.[1] It is at least equally interesting because of the new light

[1] Too simply, because it is attributed to Shakespeare as a rigid doctrine of public order on the official Tudor pattern, whilst his qualifications—in terms of the living energies that the order exists to serve—are ignored. Thus in *Troilus and Cressida* Shakespeare does not simply *endorse* Ulysses, to whom he gives the best known statement on 'degree'. See my essay on the play in *Some Shakespearean Themes*. In *The Problem of Order: Elizabethan Political Commonplaces and an Example of Shakespeare's Art* E. W. Talbert shows how far from homogeneous was Elizabethan political thought.

in which More compels the rioters to see the troublesome situation. Whatever economic motives may have lain behind the agitation, what really moves the crowd is that the Flemings and Frenchmen in their midst are 'aliens'—strangers with strange habits ('they bring in strange roots . . . we will show no mercy upon the strangers'). Now the basic appeal of More's speech is to the need for peace and order and, later, to the importance of doing as one would be done by; but the argument throughout is in terms of what actually happens to actual people, and his opening lines (in the quoted passage) are an appeal for the imaginative realization of the situation in human terms.

> . . . Imagine that you see the wretched strangers,
> Their babies at their backs, with their poor luggage,
> Plodding to the ports and coasts for transportation . . .

In those three lines the generalized abstractions of propaganda give way to the actual and specific. And this, I should claim, is Shakespeare's characteristic way of dealing with political and social situations that lend themselves only too easily to the process of over-simplification by which notions and ideas take the place of the complexities of the actual.

Shakespeare, in other words, is a poet engaged in the poet's task of retrieving words from the realm of abstraction and bringing them back to human experience in its fullness, whence they draw their life. Thus in *Henry IV* Part I he examines in terms of particular actions and particular attitudes the word 'honour', and in *Measure for Measure*, 'justice'. The ironic glance in *The Tempest* at the use of 'freedom' by those who are not free[1] is entirely in keeping with what he had been doing since, in *Henry VI*, he had made Jack Cade describe how, 'All the realm shall be in common . . . when I am king, as king I will be'. To put it in another way: Shakespeare takes an action,

[1] *The Tempest*, II, ii, 191 ff.

a situation, an attitude, and asks—What does it *mean* in terms of the actual and specific? A simple but effective example is *King John* where, in the opening scenes, the unreality of the language of diplomacy is contrasted with the solid reality of self-interest, as Faulconbridge the Bastard is there to observe. In *Henry IV*, which is so much more than a political play, the public situation is defined and judged in terms of a richly human context in which Falstaff's ragged regiment and the Cotswold conscripts are an indispensable part. And even in the comparatively simple *Henry V* Shakespeare is asking questions about the nature of the successful ruler and the conditions and consequences of a successful war, which are incapable of a simple answer. It is only the Choruses—declamatory and un-subtle—that give us the public view of the simple heroic leader and the simply glorious war. The play itself contains such things as Henry's questioning of the nature of kingly responsi-bility, some realistic glimpses of the inevitable military riff-raff and of what the war means to them, and descriptions of the miseries of war that are completely free from heroic glamour.

It is, I think, true to say that one of Shakespeare's major pre-occupations was with the distortion and falsification in political and public life that goes with excessive simplification of the issues—with the habit of abstracting from the rich complexity of the actual in the interest of an abstract notion such as 'honour' or 'policy'. It is this that gives point to *Julius Caesar* with its marked contrast between the realm of the personal, where truth between man and man resides, and the purely political and public realm. Indeed it is the attempt, common to both sides in the play, to divorce the personal from the political, that largely accounts for the sense of something monstrous in the action, the sense we have of people losing touch with reality in an impossible attempt to make 'politics' self-enclosed. And it is this same intuition of the *necessary* relation between the pol-itical and the personal that lies behind *Coriolanus*, the greatest of Shakespeare's political plays, which even in a short survey demands more than cursory attention.

In *Coriolanus* we are certainly concerned with the public world. But whereas in *Julius Caesar* the 'Roman' background served mainly to throw into relief the chief performers, here the background (misleading word) is part of the living texture of the play. This Rome, for all its handful of citizens, is densely populated, and men press upon each other in the same thick clusters as the buildings:

> stalls, bulks, windows,
> Are smother'd up, leads fill'd, and ridges hors'd
> With variable complexions . . .

It is a world where men play their public parts as soldiers, officers of state, justices and tradesmen, and the 'multiplying' people swarm in the market-place or yawn in congregations. And corresponding to the felt solidity of the city, itself an effect of poetic evocation, of imagery and allusion, is a moral density and vibrancy. Once again, honour—both the public regard that men seek and the social sanction of their actions—is a main subject of the story, and as in *Henry IV*, *Julius Caesar*, and *Troilus and Cressida* it is subjected to a radical scrutiny.

The process starts in the domestic scene (I, iii) that follows hard on the splendid 'public' opening. Here Volumnia states explicitly the articles of the faith in which—we are told often enough—she has moulded her son.

> If my son were my husband, I should freelier rejoice in that absence wherein he won honour than in the embracements of his bed where he would show most love. . . .

This honour, fame, or renown, is associated exclusively with the 'masculine' warrior qualities; and although there is no hint in the play of any under-valuing of physical bravery, we are left in no doubt of the rigidity and narrowness of the code.

In Volumnia's affirmation the 'honourable' qualities are repeatedly set over against the values of spontaneous life—

> —the breasts of Hecuba,
> When she did suckle Hector, look'd not lovlier
> Than Hector's forehead when it spit forth blood.

If ironic commentary is needed, it is supplied by her grim approbation of her grandson's mammocking of the butterfly.

In the magnificent third act, in the mounting tension in which the cleft and opposition in Rome is made palpable, there is a lull in the action whilst the patricians take counsel. In this scene the theme of 'honour' is taken up again.

> *Vol.* . . . I have heard you say,
>   Honour and policy, like unsever'd friends,
>   I' the war do grow together: grant that, and tell me
>   In peace what each of them by the other lose,
>   That they combine not there . . .
>   If it be honour in your wars to seem
>   The same you are not, which, for your best ends,
>   You adopt your policy, how is it less or worse,
>   That it shall hold companionship in peace
>   With honour, as in war, since that to both
>   It stands in like request?
> *Cor.*   Why force you this?
> *Vol.* Because that now it lies you on to speak
>   To the people; not by your own instruction,
>   Nor by the matter which your heart prompts you,
>   But with such words that are but roted in
>   Your tongue, though but bastards and syllables
>   Of no allowance to your bosom's truth.
>   Now, this no more dishonours you at all
>   Than to take in a town with gentle words,
>   Which else would put you to your fortune and
>   The hazard of much blood.
>   I would dissemble with my nature where

>   My fortunes and my friends at stake requir'd
>   I should do so in honour.

I think this is one of the few places where without irrelevance
we can describe what Shakespeare is doing in the political
terminology of a later age: he is revealing the class basis ('my
fortunes and my friends') of patrician 'honour'. But he is doing
much more than that. For what Volumnia advocates—the
passing of counterfeit coin, the use of words that are but roted
in the tongue—is nothing less than an abrogation of those
qualities of mutuality and trust on which *any* society must be
founded. There is a corroding cynicism (and the tone suggests
he is half-conscious of it) in the words with which Coriolanus
accepts his mother's prompting.

>   Pray be content:
>   Mother, I am going to the market-place;
>   Chide me no more. *I'll mountebank their loves,*
>   *Cog their hearts from them,* and come home belov'd
>   Of all the trades in Rome. . . .
>   I'll return consul,
>   Or never trust to what my tongue can do
>   I' the way of flattery further.

That Coriolanus does not in fact cog the plebeians' hearts, but
loses his temper and defies them, is nothing to the point—
which is that the structure of his habitual attitudes offers
no resistance to the corruption (there is no other word) of
Volumnia's persuading. Coriolanus's mind, as the play reveals
it to us, is accustomed to move in terms of a rigid but false anti-
thesis. Just as, for him, the only alternative to steel is the
parasite's silk (I, ix, 55), and to the warrior the eunuch (III,
ii, 112–14), so the only alternative to aggressive self-assertion
that he can think of is 'flattery'. Now the use that the word
'flattery' has for him has already been made clear; it is a way of
holding people at a distance, of refusing to admit relationship.

The condition of health for 'Rome' (for which we can substitute London or Paris) was, of course, that there should be some degree of mutuality between the different members and classes, as in the fable of the belly, placed—with some effect of irony—at the opening of the play. It is because for Coriolanus large classes of people are reduced to the category of 'it' that, without clear consciousness of the evil in the words, he can speak of 'mountebanking' the people's loves, of using deceit where deceit is monstrous.

In a sense Coriolanus's tragedy is that he cannot grow up, that, as Wyndham Lewis says, he remains a boy to the end. For although he 'obeys instinct' and submits to his mother's pleading (and there is nobility in his submission) he does not change. It is as an angry boy that he retorts to the taunt of 'boy'. That is his private tragedy; but his own failure to achieve integration is certainly not something that can be dismissed as irrelevant to public considerations. The play is an experiment in *concrete* political thinking, and one of the things that it demonstrates so superbly is that disruption in the state—the body politic—is related to individual disharmony by something more palpable than an Elizabethan trick of metaphor, that the public crisis is rooted in the personal and habitual.

ii

The reason why Shakespeare's political plays can so refresh and invigorate our own thinking is that they embody not doctrines but specific insights: they are a perpetual warning against simplification and abstraction, a solvent of mechanical and rigid formulae. Now works of genius are never purely personal, never simply the products of the individual genius (Shakespeare's achievement, as F. R. Leavis has remarked, would have been impossible if the English language had not already been there[1]), and the question I now wish to pursue is— What are the sources and conditions of the political wisdom that we find in Shakespeare's plays?

I think the Bastard in *King John* gives us a clue. His idiom, references and manner relate him not to the world of high policy that he criticises so devastatingly but to the local world —where 'St George that swinged the dragon . . . sits on his horseback at mine hostess' door', a world—like Bunyan's— where observation is direct and comment forthright. He belongs, we may say, to Stratford-on-Avon.

This is not the place, nor have I the ability, to describe in any detail the features of the small local communities of which Elizabethan England was so largely composed. There are, I think, three points that are especially relevant to an enquiry of this kind. The first is that outside the few large towns most essential goods were produced in the immediate region and there was a fairly direct relation between producer and consumer. Skill, therefore, was individual and apparent; not only had each man a necessary part to play in the economy of the social group, he played it, so to speak, in public. The second is indicated by Miss Mildred Campbell in her book on the English yeoman when she writes: 'Functions that are today performed by nurses, physicians, social workers, secretaries, real-estate agents and lawyers were among the country folk of Elizabethan and Stuart days performed by neighbours for each other.'[2] In other words, neighbourliness (which according to Miss Campbell 'stands perhaps first in the criteria by which the social and ethical standing of an individual in a country community was measured') was not simply a diffused benevolence, but was made up of specific habits, attitudes and acts. The third

[1] *For Continuity*, p. 215.
[2] Mildred Campbell, *The English Yeoman under Elizabeth and the Early Stuarts* (Yale University Press, 1942), pp. 382 ff.

point is that the towns and to a lesser extent the country parishes enjoyed a considerable degree of administrative self-sufficiency.[1] Here it is enough to recall the multifarious duties carried out by the Justices of the Peace—the maids-of-all-work of the Tudor administrative system—and, below them, by the constables, church wardens, overseers of the poor, surveyors of highways and bridges and so on. 'Parliament', says Professor Ogg, 'was a wonderful institution; but the unpaid parish constable was still more remarkable'.[2] You might find a Shallow among the J.P.s and a Dogberry among the constables, but this does not affect the significant fact that within the larger framework of national policy the local community conducted a very large share of its own business. Recent scholarship has revealed the sturdy and rooted independence of the particular community within which Shakespeare grew up; and what we know of Stratford-on-Avon is entirely in line with Professor Cheyney's description of the Elizabethan parish as 'a little world of economic, social, religious and political activity, not by any means detached from the larger spheres of hundred, county and nation, and yet to a considerable extent self-centred'.[3]

That one's neighbours were necessary, that on the whole 'we' here, not some far off 'they' there, were responsible for the common welfare, was one of the main lessons taught by life in a local community of Tudor times. Each of the small towns and parishes offered an actual working model of the organic community, which made plain by its day-to-day routine the necessity for the mutually reinforcing play of different functions. And because these functions were exercised by individuals, not im-

---

[1] The phrase is taken from A. L. Rowse's *The England of Elizabeth, Vol. I, The Structure of Society*, p. 164, where it is applied only to the towns. Both this book and the same writer's *Tudor Cornwall* contain much that is directly relevant to the discussion of local life.

[2] Quoted by Miss Campbell, *The English Yeoman*, p. 318.

[3] E. P. Cheyney, *A History of England from the Defeat of the Armada to the Death of Elizabeth*, Vol. II, p. 402.

personal organizations, and directly affected individuals, their human and moral significance was plain for all to see. I do not know whether the standard of public morality in Shakespeare's time was higher or lower than in our own (in some respects, as in the treatment of criminals and unfortunates, it was notably lower). All I wish to remark is that when the workings of society are directly exposed one is in less danger of harbouring the cant and clap-trap that sometimes result from thinking about social problems too exclusively in abstractions and general terms. Just as the basis of Shakespeare's verse, even at its most subtle and far-reaching, is the common language, so at the basis of his profoundest comments on man in society is the habit of judging public affairs in terms of their specific human causes and consequences, learnt in the school of the small local community.

It is to reflections such as these that we are led by pondering the nature of Shakespeare's political wisdom; but it is plain that we cannot stop there. We cannot attribute to 'social life' alone—to social life considered simply as a working arrangement—the insights and values that are active within it. Some forms of social organization may be more favourable than others to the fostering of values in which life finds its meaning. But when we consider more deeply, when we see society not as if it were a static arrangement but as a way of life, then it becomes clear that social life is not self-determining but is shaped by non-material factors such as the moral and religious traditions by which its members live. Shakespeare, I have said, sees social relationships, political problems and the like in terms of direct dealing between individuals. When inessentials are stripped away, events on the public stage are shown to be very similar to events on the narrower stage of the local community where Shakespeare learnt to see with such uncompromising directness. But what you see, in this sense, depends very largely on the values you hold to. ('The wise man,' said Blake, 'sees not the same tree as the fool.') Behind

Shakespeare's direct vision, and partly at least determining it, is a tradition of thought which—still keeping to my visual metaphors—directs the attention and gives depth and focus to the scene.

For some knowledge of the tradition of political thought in Shakespeare's day the literary student must turn to the expert. Professor A. P. d'Entrèves, who has put a small volume of political writings by S. Thomas Aquinas within the reach of the general student and who has shown elsewhere the influence of medieval ideas on Hooker, comments on Aquinas' use of the expression *homo naturaliter est animal politicum et sociale*. 'What is interesting', he says, 'is the emphasis which is laid upon the social character of politics. Man is a political animal because he is a social being. This means that the State must have its roots in social experience, that it cannot be, or cannot be solely, the creation of human will. The State is not a work of art, but a historical product. It is the highest expression of human fellowship.' For Aquinas and the medieval thinkers generally there was, of course, no question of the 'absolute' state; both the idea of the eternal destiny of the individual and the idea of the supremacy of law stood in the way of any such notion. Yet the State was not merely a result of the Fall; it was the condition of normal individual development. 'The integration of the individual in the whole', says Professor d'Entrèves, 'must be conceived as an enlargement and an enrichment of his personality, not as a degradation to the mere function of a part without a value of its own. Above all, the difference between the end of the individual and that of the whole does not imply a difference in the standards by which both can and must be judged. Ultimately these ends are one and the same.' In other words, to put it bluntly, 'Politics are subordinate to Ethics'.[1]

Historians of thought are agreed as to the continued vitality

[1] Aquinas, *Selected Political Writings*, ed. with an Introduction by A. P. d'Entrèves and translated by J. G. Dawson, Introduction, pp. xv, xix, xxx.

of this tradition in the sixteenth century.[1] It was challenged both by developments in the practical sphere and by the emergence of a quite different kind of political thinking, but it was still alive. Even as students of literature we need to know that in the age of Shakespeare there was available a tradition of political thought older than the Machiavellian 'grammar of power', a tradition that refused to abstract 'politics' from the rich body of total human experience and that directly encouraged the assessment of politics in terms of human actuality and the good for man.

In making these observations I have, of course, been trespassing in fields not my own. But perhaps the art of intelligent trespassing is an art that universities, where so many 'special fields' are cultivated, should foster more than they do. If the student of literature needs the historian it is at least equally clear that the historian of ideas—especially of political and social ideas—cannot dispense with the 'literary' evidence. Indeed, what I have next to observe—as I continue to cast about for the living background of Shakespeare's political insights—is the impossibility of making any sharp distinction between the tradition of 'literature' on the one hand and the literary tradition of political and social teaching and satire on the other.

One of the great central masterpieces of the fourteenth century is *The Vision of Piers Plowman*, which amply illustrates my

[1] 'The Renaissance may or may not represent a really new beginning in philosophy and science, it did not do so in political ideas and forms.'— R. W. and A. J. Carlyle, *A History of Mediaeval Political Theory in the West*, Vol. V, p. 2. 'We shall not fully understand Tudor minds unless we recognize their kinship with medieval minds. The political behaviour of Tudor statesmen was often enough stark, ruthless, and amoral: it would have shocked the more devout of medieval rulers. Nevertheless these Tudor statesmen paid lip-service at the very least to all the moral platitudes of medieval thought; and the intellectual framework within which sixteenth-century thinkers constructed their political philosophy was a framework accepted, often uncritically, from medieval schoolmen.'—Christopher Morris, *Political Thought in England: Tyndale to Hooker*, pp. 5-6. See also J. W. Allen, *A History of Political Thought in the Sixteenth Century*, Part II, chap. III, and A. P. d'Entrèves, *The Medieval Contribution to Political Thought*.

point. *Piers Plowman* is an imaginative vision of life; it is poetry, and it rises again and again to the level of great poetry; but it is not just literature as one tends to conceive literature. It is directly didactic, and both in substance and method it belongs with the vernacular sermons of the fourteenth century. It is in some ways, as Professor Owst has shown, 'the quintessence of English medieval preaching'.[1] In relation to the tradition we are considering its significance is threefold. In the first place, its social teaching is inseparable from its moral content: social, economic and political activity is presented as good or bad behaviour to one's neighbours, to the community at large, and in the sight of God; the king and his counsellors are judged by the same standards of truth and righteousness as hypocritical friars and cheating innkeepers. Secondly, all proceeds by way of specific comment and specific illustration, so that although the characters who exemplify the different moral qualities may be lightly sketched they are as vividly alive as Bunyan's.

> 'Yea, baw!' quoth a brewer,   'I will not be ruled,
> By Jesu! for all your jangling,   according to justice,
> Nor according to Conscience, by Christ!   for I can sell
> Both dregs and draff,   and draw at one hole
> Thick ale and thin ale;   and that is my kind,
> And not to hack after holiness;   hold thy tongue, Conscience!'[2]

And finally, behind the grasp of particulars is a philosophy of life—firm in the cardinal points of Christian faith, exploratory and personal in the concern to illuminate with charity much that the contemporary conscience was either content to ignore or prepared to judge more harshly. It is in the light of his Christian philosophy that Langland 'places' his examples of various vices, and—to make one more connexion with what I have said of

---

[1] G. R. Owst, *Literature and Pulpit in Medieval England*, p. 549. (Quoted from the same writer's *Preaching in Medieval England*, p. 295.)

[2] *The Vision of William Concerning Piers the Plowman*, ed. W. W. Skeat, B. Passus, XIX, ll. 394–399, or C. Passus, XXII, ll. 392–403.

Shakespeare—unless he had placed them so firmly it is unlikely that he would have *seen* them so clearly: the seeing is inseparable from the spiritual values and moral qualities to which he is committed.

It should, I think, be obvious why I have invoked Langland in this attempt to place Shakespeare's political plays within a larger tradition. A literary tradition is more than a matter of conscious influences and direct connexions, and Mr Christopher Dawson is right to name both Bunyan and Blake, neither of whom had read a word of *Piers Plowman*, as spiritual descendants of Langland.[1] More obviously, though not more surely, *Piers Plowman* relates to the vernacular sermons, to the mystery plays and the moralities; and we must include sixteenth-century sermons like Latimer's and those social moralities of the sixteenth century of the kind of Lindsay's *Ane Satyre of the Thre Estaitis*—a kind that continued until it was absorbed into the Elizabethan drama. The tradition in question is determined by a basic assumption about the kind of thing that literature does, a refusal to distinguish 'literature' from a direct 'criticism of life'. It is also, as *Piers Plowman* has served to remind us, a tradition of expression, of colloquial vigour and homely concrete illustration. It is the English version of something that is heard in other literatures, for in it speaks the voice of the countryman with his rooted distrust of the merely verbal, of what the fantastical Armado in *Love's Labour's Lost* calls 'the sweet smoke of rhetoric'. We have all laughed at Costard in that play when he opens his fist to see how much Armado has tipped him with his grandiose, 'There is remuneration':—'Now will I look to his remuneration. Remuneration! Oh!—that's the Latin word for three farthings.' But Costard here is employing a manner that lends itself to serious as well as to comic use. '*Corporal infliction*', said Cobbett, quoting a phrase from the Mutiny Act of 1811—'that is to say ...*flogging*. Why do you mince the matter? Why not name the

---

[1] Christopher Dawson, *Medieval Religion*, p. 194.

thing?'[1] Go back two and a half centuries, to Bishop Latimer in 1549 preaching before King Edward VI and adapting to his own times Isaiah's denunciation of unjust princes and magistrates: 'He calleth princes thieves. What! princes thieves? ... Did they stand by the highway side? Did they rob, or break open any man's house or door? No, no; that is a gross kind of thieving. They were princes; they had a prince-like kind of thieving. *Omnes diligunt munera*: "they all love bribes". Bribing is a princely kind of thieving. They will be waged by the rich, either to give sentence against the poor, or to put off the poor man's causes. This is the noble theft of princes and of magistrates. They are bribe takers. Nowadays they call them gentle rewards: let them leave their colouring, and call them by their christian name, bribes.'[2]— 'Let them leave their colouring.' 'Why not name the thing?'— The note is the same. Cobbett was a peasant; Latimer the son of a Leicestershire yeoman. A few years after Latimer preached before the king, some ten years before Shakespeare was born, in the anonymous morality play *Respublica*, much of the criticism of social abuses is put into the mouth of an old countryman— he is called 'People'—who has the same distrust of abstract words that can hide reality. When Avarice, disguised as Policy, asserts that he does nothing but compass the welfare of the commonwealth, People retorts:

> I say then thee went too far a compass about.
> For some good might ha' been done in all this season . . .
> Five or six year ago I had four kine to my pale;
> And at this present hour, I am scarce worth a good cowtail.
> Compassing? ha! gentleman! call you this same
>   compassing?[3]

---

[1] *The Opinions of William Cobbett*, ed. by G. D. H. and Margaret Cole, p. 222.

[2] Latimer, *Sermons*, 'Third Sermon preached before King Edward VI', Everyman edn. p. 119.

[3] *Respublica* (in '*Lost*' Tudor Plays, ed. J. S. Farmer, or ed. for E.E.T.S. by W. W. Greg), IV, iii.

POETRY, POLITICS, AND THE ENGLISH TRADITION

Four cows in your yard are better than fine words that butter no parsnips. It is because the Bastard in Shakespeare's *King John* is one of those who refuse to be 'bethump'd with words' that he can expose so effectively the workings of 'that smooth-faced gentleman, tickling Commodity'. The Bastard is very far indeed from representing the whole of Shakespeare's genius, but he stands for something essential in it. With his vivid colloquial speech he reminds us that the tradition of social realism had at its disposal a language that expressed the specific and particular more readily than the abstract and the general.[1] And he will serve to remind us that a vigorous language, itself an incitement to clarity of vision, is an integral part of a living tradition and a healthy culture.

Before drawing to an end I should like to remind you that my attempt to indicate a context for Shakespeare's political plays has been offered not only for its intrinsic interest, but as an example of the possible range of literary study. Certainly literature is more than an illustration of social history or the history of ideas. It is made up of particular works of art, and the first and essential business of the student of literature is to grasp these in their uniqueness, to respond to them with all the imaginative power of which he is capable. But equally (it seems to me) the study of literature cannot be separated from the study

[1] 'They [Cervantes and Boccaccio] had not to deal with the world in such great masses that it could only be represented to their minds by figures and generalizations. Everything that their minds ran on came to them vivid with the colour of the senses, and when they wrote it was out of their own rich experience, and they found their symbols of expression in things that they had known all their life long. Their very words were more vigorous than ours, for their phrases came from a common mint, from the market, or the tavern, or from the great poets of a still older time. It is the change, that followed the Renaissance and was completed by newspaper government and the scientific movement, that has brought upon us all these phrases and generalizations, made by minds that would grasp what they have never seen.'—W. B. Yeats, 'The Irish Dramatic Movement', *Plays and Controversies*, pp. 96–7; reprinted in Yeats's *Explorations*, selected by Mrs W. B. Yeats.

71

of society, of a way of life, and of the ideas men live by. In this small demonstration we started from Shakespeare's characteristic insistence on the relation of the political and the personal, that vivid sense of actuality in his plays that no generalized political notion is ever allowed to obscure, and we found ourselves invoking, among other things, the medieval insistence on the human and moral basis of politics, the medieval recognition of an authority higher than the political. To what extent Shakespeare was consciously influenced by political ideas deriving from medieval thinkers I do not know. It is, I think, a matter for further investigation. I have been content to point out that such ideas were available to his generation, and that the social conditions of sixteenth-century England, the vivid life of small local communities, had much in common with the conditions that helped to determine the political and social thought of the Middle Ages. Even as students of literature, even, that is, as people who do not know as much about history and political philosophy as we should like, we find ourselves inquiring about these things and pondering them, trying to see their significance in the light of what we know of other traditions and other societies and from our own direct experience. And it seems to me an indication of the humanizing value of literary studies that an attempt to understand, say, *Coriolanus*, should at least bring into view ways of thinking about politics and society that do not begin with the question of power, and forms of social life in which direct relationships are obviously more important than impersonal techniques. Merely to begin to think on these lines is, for the student, not only to learn something about the nature of a literary tradition, but to become aware of the presentness of the past and of the relevance of literature to life.

My example, I say, is only an example, and I certainly do not expect all university English teachers to share my interest in the social bases of literature and its social and political implications. The special interests of D. G. James, my predecessor in the

Winterstoke Chair, led him to investigate the bearings of philosophy on literature and the philosophic implications of poetry and criticism in those books by which he is widely known. And in addition to these more public services, Professor James, in his teaching, certainly opened up prospects within which English studies revealed a richer significance. And English teachers with other interests will have other ways of promoting that cross-fertilization on which—at all events in the Humanities —the life of special studies depends.

Yet I cannot avoid the conviction that—in this age of confusion which also shows signs of being an age of radical re-thinking of old problems—the line of reflection that I have indicated has a very special significance. What I have tried to emphasize, in relation to politics and social thought, is the value of a literature that refuses to deal in abstractions. M. Gabriel Marcel, in his interesting volume of thoughts on the present age translated as *Men against Humanity*, has some valuable things to say about the relation between the spirit of abstraction and propaganda, resentment, fanaticism, and mass violence; and it is perhaps in our thinking about social and international relations that we are most in danger of succumbing to a dangerous unreality. Anything that helps us, as Shakespeare's political plays help us, to bring these matters back to the level of the human and specific should have an obvious contemporary value. M. Marcel also reminds us that admiration, love and creativeness exist only in the realm of the concrete; and perhaps we may allow this great and obvious truth to lead us away from politics to considerations about literature that lie far outside the limits of this lecture. 'Art', says Yeats, 'bids us touch and taste and hear and see the world, and shrinks from what Blake calls mathematic form, from every abstract thing. . . .'[1] I think that is true; but it is only part of the truth. For the opposite of abstraction is not only physical immediacy, it is full imaginative realization, in which

[1] W. B. Yeats, *Essays*, p. 362.

73

sensuous awareness works to the same end as sympathy and intelligence. And if the poet is what Wordsworth called him, 'a rock of defence for human nature', it is because poetry, indeed all great imaginative literature, rescues man from abstractions and brings him back continually to the specific possibilities of creative living. It is to the service of poetry as a source of creative insight and understanding in the realm of the actual, where men of all kinds can meet, that we English teachers bring the resources of literary criticism and literary scholarship.

The Strange Case
of Christopher Marlowe

MARLOWE'S life and works together present one of the strangest puzzles in our literary history. Of his life we know enough to make the blanks and uncertainties tantalizing. We cannot even trace with certainty the development of his thought and art; for although it is probable that *Tamburlaine* was Marlowe's first work for the London stage the chronological order of the other plays is still open to dispute. *Dr Faustus*, which some regard as the culmination of his short career, is placed by others near its beginning. The text of that play, as is well known, exists in two versions, and although it seems likely that the later of the two is nearer to the original, we do not know how much of the original was Marlowe's, or who—if anyone—collaborated with him. Even more important, critical opinion concerning the nature and the value of the plays is sharply divided.

> Sunrise and thunder fired and shook the skies
> That saw the sun-god Marlowe's opening eyes.

If there are none today to share Swinburne's raptures about Marlowe as the herald of a new humanism, it is still possible to present him, in a sober study, as a serious and impassioned proponent of free thought and rational disbelief—'an heir of all the ages of protest against Christianity and a voice for the inarticulate and nameless of his own day'. On the other hand there are equally sober, equally well documented studies that tell us the precise opposite: however much Marlowe may have sympathized with the arrogant individualism of his heroes, the sequence of plays traces, with increasing objectivity, 'the inevitable impoverishment of Renaissance humanism'. Such differences of opinion do more than reflect conflicting attitudes towards the Renaissance; they spring from radically opposed critical judgments concerning the nature of Marlowe's achievement. And when we put the critics on one side and try once more to make a personal estimate of the plays—asking ourselves what kind of thing they are and how they demand to be taken, how they stand in relation to other works of literature and what nourishment for the imagination they contain—then, unless we have a very strong *parti pris*, we are likely to find ourselves veering with each fresh reconsideration of the major plays. That at all events has been my fate in preparing this lecture, and I am able to bring nothing to this quatercentenary celebration but an attempt to account for perplexity; an attempt which may perhaps, however, help to promote understanding of the nature and the limitations of Marlowe's genius.

i

The main facts of Marlowe's life can be briefly told. He was born at Canterbury in 1564, the first son and second child of John Marlowe of the Shoemakers' Guild. Shortly before his fifteenth birthday he was admitted as a scholar to the King's School. Early in 1580 he was admitted to Corpus Christi College, Cambridge, as the holder of one of the scholarships founded by Matthew Parker, Master of the College from 1544 to 1553 and later Archbishop of Canterbury. He retained the scholarship for six years, which means both that his behaviour was satisfactory—he took the B.A. degree in 1584—and that he was regarded as a candidate for holy orders. In June 1587, when Marlowe had supplicated for, but had not yet received, his M.A. degree, the Privy Council addressed to the University the following letter:

Whereas it was reported that Christopher Morley was determined to have gone beyond the sea to Rheims and there to remain, their

Lordships thought good to certify that he had no such intent, but that in all his actions he had behaved himself orderly and discreetly, whereby he had done her Majesty good service and deserved to be rewarded for his faithful dealing. Their Lordships' request was that the rumour thereof should be allayed by all possible means, and that he should be furthered in the degree he was to take this next commencement; because it was not her Majesty's pleasure that any one employed as he had been in matters touching the benefit of his country should be defamed by those that are ignorant in th'ffairs he went about.

Dr Leslie Hotson, who established that the letter refers to Marlowe, envisages the poet, 'supported by his former employers, the Privy Council, wresting his master's degree from the cold and hostile Cambridge authorities'. The grounds of that hostility we do not know, though the mention of Rheims suggests a suspicion of Roman Catholic leanings. We do not know the nature of the 'matters touching the benefit of his country' in which Marlowe had been employed. Nor do we know whether he continued his discreet services to the government. It may be noted however that it is probable that he spent the last months of his life at the country home of Thomas Walsingham, uncle of Sir Francis Walsingham, and that Robert Poley, who was with Marlowe at the time of his death, had been employed by Sir Francis Walsingham as a spy at the time of the Babington conspiracy. After the award of the M.A. degree in July 1587, Marlowe was soon well known in London literary circles, with a reputation for reckless talk about religion, and it seems that he knew Sir Walter Raleigh and the members of Raleigh's circle. But there are few hard facts until the last month of his life. In May 1593 he was summoned to appear before the Privy Council, presumably as a witness. On May 30 he was stabbed to death by Ingram Frizer in an eating-house at Deptford. The coroner's jury found that the quarrel had arisen about the reckoning, and that Frizer had acted in self-defence. Meanwhile Thomas Kyd, whose rooms had been searched in connexion with some recent disturbances, had protested that papers containing dangerous opinions found with his own were not his but Marlowe's. He later elaborated on this, saying that he went in some fear of Marlowe 'in regard of his rashness in attempting soden pryvie iniuries to men'. At about the same time an informer, Richard Baines, sent to the Privy Council 'A note containing the opinion of one Christopher Marly concerning his damnable judgment of religion and scorn of God's word'. It is not known now much of what Kyd reported in a panic, or of what Baines reported for some motive of his own, corresponded to Marlowe's actual opinions, though it seems likely that he was accustomed to make provocative and 'atheist' remarks in all companies. Marlowe was buried at Deptford on June 1, 1593, and four years later Thomas Beard, in *The Theatre of God's Judgements*, adduced, with some inaccuracy, the manner of his death as a warning to atheists and epicures.[1]

Facts of this kind however tell us little more than that Marlowe was in some ways an outsider, one who did not easily find a place in the established society of his day. But how did that society appear to the man who experienced it in his living consciousness? There is evidence enough that he regarded much of what he saw with exasperation and contempt; and before we turn to the plays we may dwell for a moment on some features of that complex and remote Elizabethan world. It is doubtful whether Cambridge did much for Marlowe beyond giving him access to a good library. Ruled by an oligarchy, divided into factions, remote from the world of action yet offering a foothold for worldly corruption, it was not a great home of learning, nor a place where exceptional talent could be sure of reward. Scholarship had suffered from the religious strife of the mid-

---

[1] For the information in this paragraph I have drawn on Leslie Hotson's *The Death of Christopher Marlowe* and the *Life* by C. F. Tucker Brooke in the Methuen edition of Marlowe's Works (ed. R. H. Case).

century; Roman Catholic and Protestant scholars alike had been compelled to go abroad, and much energy was expended in petty controversy. What a contemporary referred to as 'these fanatical contests about the surplice and the cap' (amid which 'the time once bestowed upon the arts and sciences' was 'frittered away in frivolous disputes') had died down by 1580. But theology, narrow and intolerant, remained the dominant study; and although rhetoric and logic retained their medieval pre-eminence, the mathematical sciences had no place in the formal curriculum, such knowledge as there was of cosmography and astronomy had no relation to contemporary discovery, history and linguistic studies were at a low ebb. By the end of the century, according to Bass Mullinger, 'the enquiring spirit of the Renaissance had again given place to something like medieval credulity'. It is hard to resist the conclusion that Arnold's 'national glow of life and thought'—which, he said, made possible the literary achievement of the Elizabethan age—was somewhat dimly reflected in Marlowe's Cambridge, where, it must be remembered, he spent rather more than half his adult life.[1]

As for the greater world that Marlowe saw when he 'cast the scholar off' and rejected a clerical career, there is only one aspect of it that can be touched on here. In *Edward II*, Spencer Junior advises the ambitious ex-scholar Baldock:

> 'Tis not a black coat and a little band,
> A velvet-cap'd cloak, faced before with serge,
> And smelling to a nosegay all the day . . .
> Or looking downward with your eyelids close,
> And saying, 'Truly, an't may please your honour',

[1] I have drawn on the standard history of the University by James Bass Mullinger, *The University of Cambridge*, Vol. II, *From the Royal Injunctions of 1535 to the Accession of Charles I*. H. C. Porter's *Reformation and Reaction in Tudor Cambridge* gives a far more lively and intimate picture of the University, but it does not seem to me to demand any substantial revision of the general impression of the University *c*. 1580 obtained from the older work.

Can get you any favour with great men;
You must be proud, bold, pleasant, resolute,
And now and then stab, as occasion serves.

This, besides providing an example of the dramatist's best
laconic manner, opens a window on Marlowe's world. To trace
the ramifications of Sir Francis Walsingham's activities as head
of the secret service (with which Marlowe was perhaps connected) is to learn something of the devious violence with which
Elizabethan state power was underpinned.[1] Violence less devious
was enacted at the Tower and Tyburn and elsewhere; and
although much of this could be defended on grounds of national
security, a similar ruthlessness inspired both the struggle for
wealth and power of Elizabeth's courtiers at home and the
mercantile struggle to exploit the new sources of wealth abroad.
It was with some restraint that Marx described the methods of
that phase of capitalist activity as 'anything but idyllic'.[2] It was
Shakespeare's Faulconbridge who jauntily supplied a motto for
the age:

Since kings break faith upon commodity,
Gain be my lord, for I will worship thee.

This thumb-nail sketch is of course grossly over-simplified;
and rapacity is not peculiar to any age. My point however is not
only that these were in fact obtrusive features of the world that
Marlowe knew, but that a ruthless self-seeking was linked by

[1] See Conyers Read, *Mr Secretary Walsingham and the Policy of Queen
Elizabeth*, Chapters XI and XII.

[2] *See Capital*, translated by Eden and Cedar Paul (Everyman edition),
Vol. II, Part VII, Chapter 24, 'Primary Accumulation'. I do not know that
any of Marx's instances of rapacity have ever been contradicted. When, on
pp. 833-4, one reads the following, one begins to suspect the existence of
a Dutch translation of *The Jew of Malta*!—'Wishing to get possession of
Malacca, the Dutch bribed the Portuguese governor of the town, promising
to pay him the sum of £21,875 as the price of his treason. When he admitted
them within the walls, in the year 1641, as per bargain, they hastened to his
house and assassinated him, wishing to "abstain" from payment.'

complex gradations to an official piety altogether too deficient in self-questioning. It was not Marx but an unusually well-qualified literary scholar who said, 'Religion is soon shaped to fit the peculiar wishes of a rising capitalist nation. Protestantism, particularly in its Calvinist branches, develops into a faith supporting property and the prudential virtues. Christ and the New Testament become the bulwarks of trade and commerce.'[1] If I may put it so, there was a large element of the Victorian in the Elizabethan mind. The self-righteous self-assurance of a world that offered small resistance to drives for power and riches might well provoke exasperation in a mind that was not afraid of asking radical questions:—'What right had Caesar to the empery?' In these circumstances the intelligent outsider who was also a born writer might do one of two things. He might identify himself with the expansive drives of his contemporaries, magnifying them and stripping them of any conventional protective justifications. Or he might—and by the same process of stripping—expose them for what they were.

> Now tell me, worldlings, underneath the sun
> If greater falsehood ever has bin done?

My reading of the plays is that Marlowe attempted to do both, and that for the most part he was never quite clear about his own purposes.

ii

Marlowe's plays deal with power and pride and individual self-assertion. What, as an artist, has he to say of these matters? Does he simply endorse, or does he probe and clarify, that 'unrestrained individualism' which is rightly regarded as his main,

---

[1] Louis B. Wright, *Middle-Class Culture in Elizabethan England*, p. 268.

his obsessive, theme? I have already indicated my own opinion; but the question is too complicated to admit an easy answer, and I propose to approach it indirectly. Since in art 'substance' only exists in and through 'form', we may obtain some illumination by considering a particular feature of Marlowe's blank verse. In *The Massacre at Paris* the Guise reveals his ambitions:

> Now Guise begins those deep-engender'd thoughts
> To burst abroad those never-dying flames
> Which cannot be extinguished but by blood.
> Oft have I levell'd, and at last have learn'd
> That peril is the chiefest way to happiness,
> And resolution honour's fairest aim.
> What glory is there in a common good,
> That hangs for every peasant to achieve?
> That like I best, that flies beyond my reach.
> Set me to scale the high Pyramides,
> And thereon set the diadem of France;
> I'll either rend it with my nails to naught,
> Or mount the top with my aspiring wings,
> Although my downfall be the deepest hell.
> For this I wake, when others think I sleep,
> For this I wait, that scorns attendance else;
> For this, my quenchless thirst, whereon I build,
> Hath often pleaded kindred to the King;
> For this, this head, this heart, this hand, and sword,
> Contrives, imagines, and fully executes,
> Matters of import aimed at by many,
> Yet understood by none;
> For this, hath heaven engender'd me of earth;
> For this, this earth sustains my body's weight,
> And with this weight I'll counterpoise a crown,
> Or with seditions weary all the world. . . .

The Massacre is, admittedly, a very bad play; but—to mis-quote Coleridge—if you met these lines running wild in the deserts of Arabia, you would instantly exclaim 'Marlowe'. It is not only

that the Guise provides a motto for so many of Marlowe's
heroes ('That like I best that flies beyond my reach'), the verse
itself—with its constant superlatives, over-emphasis, and hyperbole—is characteristically Marlovian. The exaggeration and
expansiveness are not in the least critical—as you can see by
putting the passage beside comparable speeches of Ben Jonson's
Sejanus: it simply flows with the minimum of control. Marlowe,
as we shall see, had other ways of writing, and what he achieved
in blank verse, at his best, has been rightly praised; but the
passage quoted does fairly represent a quality found in almost
all his plays—a free-flowing impetuousness that somehow fails
to be transformed into the energies of art.[1]

It was a valuable remark of T. S. Eliot's that 'no artist produces great art by a deliberate attempt to express his personality.
He expresses his personality indirectly through concentrating
upon a task . . .'. What I have called the energies of art spring
from a disciplined concentration: they do their work most
effectively when the artist's primary impulses are subject to a
certain resistance—a resistance that may indeed be assimilated
and overcome, but that is in some ways similar to the resistance
offered to the sculptor by the intrinsic nature of wood and stone.
The analogy is suggestive rather than exact, and different poets
find different formal disciplines. They may practise their art by
imitating chosen masters. Dante and Shakespeare were skilled
in the rhetorical arts of language of their times. (The figure of
Beatrice begins her ever-growing symbolic life in the *Vita*

---

[1] J. A. Symonds, who writes well of Marlowe's achievement in blank
verse, has some interesting comments on the poet's handling of Virgil's text
in *Dido*, II, I ('the exaggerated, almost spasmodic attempt made to heighten
the tragic tension of each situation').—*Shakespeare's Predecessors*, Chapter
XV. Tucker Brooke's notes to the same scene in his edition of *Dido* provide
some further examples. In the well-known simile borrowed by Marlowe
from Spenser—'Like to an almond tree ymounted high . . .' (2 *Tamburlaine*,
IV, iii, 119)—the lines added to the original make the comparison even more
diffuse and inappropriate than it is in *The Faerie Queene* (I, vii, 32).

83

Nuova, which to modern eyes can seem, at times, an almost pedantic exercise; and of Shakespeare's Sonnets Keats said, 'They seem to be full of fine things said unintentionally—in the intensity of working out conceits'.) The Metaphysical poets carried into poetry some of the sternly patterned techniques of religious meditation. Emily Dickinson hammered out her concentrated expressive forms with the help of a manual of hymn-book metrics.[1] In great works of art, therefore, there is a certain doubleness. They extend the area of consciousness, but in such a way that their symbolic forms activate a wider area of experience than their authors, or anyone else, could express in conceptual, non-symbolic language. But it is by the way of artifice that they enlist what is pre-conscious and inarticulate, drawing—as Dryden has it—'the sleeping images of things *towards the light*' (my italics). In Marlowe this subtle balance between 'reason', deliberate craftsmanship or formal artifice and the unconscious or partly conscious affective life from which reason springs, is upset. His work does not only enlist, it is partly at the mercy of, unconscious drives. That is why Symonds could say of Marlowe's 'colossal personifications' that 'we feel them to be day-dreams of their maker's deep desires'.[2]

It is important to be clear on this point, for the issues are sometimes clouded by the assumption that these 'embodiments of a craving for illimitable power', whether or not they are meant to be admired, are in fact heroic. It is a questionable assumption; how questionable we are unlikely to know so long as we continue to see these figures exclusively in relation to some Herculean prototype or to the Renaissance quest for power and knowledge in the real world of thought and action. In the curious prologue to the action in *Dido, Queen of Carthage*, Marlowe embroiders

---

[1] See Louis L. Martz, *The Poetry of Meditation*; T. H. Johnson, *Emily Dickinson: a Critical Biography*.

[2] *Shakespeare's Predecessors*, Chapter XV; quoted by Raymond Mortimer in an article in the *Sunday Times*, February 2, 1964.

freely on a hint from Virgil. Jupiter is dandling upon his knee
the youthful Ganymede.

> What is't, sweet wag, I should deny thy youth? . . .
> Sit on my knee, and call for thy content,
> Control proud Fate, and cut the thread of Time:
> Why, are not all the gods at thy command,
> And heaven and earth the bounds of thy delight?
> Vulcan shall dance to make thee laughing sport,
> And my nine daughters sing when thou art sad;
> From Juno's bird I'll pluck her spotted pride,
> To make thee fans wherewith to cool thy face;
> And Venus' swans shall shed their silver down,
> To sweeten out the slumbers of thy bed. . . .

It is with unmistakeable—and characteristic—gusto that Marlowe paints his picture of indulged infancy. And what is promised to the baby-figure Ganymede ('that wanton female boy')
is precisely the unlimited power, gained without effort—'To
ask and have, command and be obeyed'—that enters so largely
into the enormous fantasy of *Tamburlaine the Great*.

The element of fantasy, of day-dream, in *Tamburlaine* is
recognized in most accounts of Marlowe's work, but perhaps
not the nature and significance of the fantasy. The scenes of
violence, presented or described, with which Marlowe indulges
himself and his audience—Bajazeth and his empress in the cage,
Bajazeth as Tamburlaine's footstool, the kings drawing the
chariot—are not only exaggerated, they bear no relation to the
cruelty that men actually inflict on each other, as the blinding of
Gloucester in *Lear* brings to a head all the latent cruelty of the
world. They are spectacular, and their function—crudely
enough—is to say. 'Look at me, doing this!'

> *Techelles.* Methinks I see kings kneeling at his feet,
>   And he with frowning brows and fiery looks
>   Spurning their crowns from off their captive heads. . . .
> *Tamburlaine.* Nobly resolv'd, sweet friends and followers!

Tamburlaine, it seems, can never have enough of being looked at.

> And with our sun-bright armour, as we march,
> We'll chase the stars from heaven and dim their eyes
> That stand and muse at our admired arms.

> Then in my coach, like Saturn's royal son
> Mounted his shining chariot gilt with fire,
> And drawn with princely eagles through the path
> Pav'd with bright crystal and enchas'd with stars,
> When all the gods stand gazing at his pomp,
> So will I ride through Samarcanda streets. . . .

For the gazing gods we may substitute parents and other grown-ups whose favours can be won for the powerless and demanding child by almost magical means:

> To ask and have, command and be obeyed;
> When looks breed love, with looks to gain the prize.

The power that is expressed through Tamburlaine has no gradations; it knows no obstacles, and it is immediate in effect.

> Draw forth thy sword, thou mighty man at arms,
> Intending but to raze my charmed skin,
> And Jove himself will stretch his hand from heaven
> To ward the blow, and shield me safe from harm.

> . . . such a star hath influence in his sword
> As rules the skies and countermands the gods. . . .

> I speak it, and my words are oracles.

None of this has any relation to the real extension of human capacity in the sixteenth century; it is simply the regressive craving for effortless and unlimited power. Tamburlaine's titanic boast—

> I hold the Fates bound fast in iron chains,
> And with my hand turn Fortune's wheel about

86

—is a precise echo of what was promised to the obviously infantile Ganymede.[1]

iii

Clearly if this were all that Marlowe had to offer we should not be bothering with him four hundred years after his birth, and I must now face directly what seems to me the central puzzle of his plays. For Marlowe, with all his limitations, does have a creative energy that keeps his plays alive as something other than pieces in the Elizabethan museum. He is important, moreover, not only because of the unusual vigour with which he pursues his day-dreams, but because with part of his mind he knew those day-dreams for what they were.

---

[1] Anyone qualified to pursue a psycho-analytic approach would find much of interest in the plays. Marlowe is of course notably preoccupied with displacing the father—'The thirst of reign. . . . That caused the eldest son of heavenly Ops To thrust his doting father from his chair . . .'—though I suspect that the relevant psychology may be Suttie's rather than Freud's. Further unconscious material is indicated by recurrent words and images. Marlowe's fondness for the word 'admire'—to gaze at with wonder—and for the imagery of fired buildings is commented on by Tucker Brooke in his notes to *Dido*, III, ii, 72, and IV, iv, 92; and in the *Life* prefixed to *Dido* this perceptive editor remarks that it is 'strange that . . . [Marlowe] should recur with such ruthlessness to the idea of burning topless towers, of firing crazed buildings, and enforcing "the papal towers to kiss the lowly earth" '. Perhaps not altogether strange. A recent study of some youthful fire-raisers found that most of the children observed had severe rage reactions. The fire-raising seems to have served various purposes: to externalize (internal) destructive threats, and so gain a measure of control over them; to identify with an imagined aggressor; in some way to achieve contact with the father, conceived as food-giver and nurse; and, finally, to ensure that by hook or by crook they would be *seen*.—'A Re-Evaluation of the Psychodynamics of Firesetting', by Kaufman, Heims and Reiser, *American Journal of Orthopsychiatry*, XXXI, 1961, pp. 123–36. I owe this reference to Professor D. Russell Davis.

I have commented on the free-flow of much of Marlowe's verse. But besides the note of unresisted self-indulgence there is, almost from the first, another note, which Dr Bradbrook has defined so well in relation to *Hero and Leander*[1]: it is the note of dry and sardonic detachment and irony that blends with and qualifies the exuberance.

> Where'er I come the fatal sisters sweat,
> And grisly death, by running to and fro
> To do their ceaseless homage to my sword. . . .

That flicker of caricature comes from the last scene of the first Part of *Tamburlaine*, and together with Zenocrate's moving lament for 'the Turk and his great emperess'—

> Ah, mighty Jove and holy Mahomet,
> Pardon my love! O pardon his contempt
> Of earthly fortune and respect of pity—

it perhaps does something to put in a sane perspective the prevailing megalomania. In Part II, as is well known, there is rather more to qualify Tamburlaine's own view of himself. The cowardly son, Calyphas, has a glimmer of not quite Falstaffian realism:

> The bullets fly at random where they list;
> And should I go and kill a thousand men,
> I were as soon rewarded with a shot,
> And sooner far than he that never fights.

And the death of Zenocrate—'I fare, my lord, as other empresses' —does act as a touchstone of reality: as Theridamas is allowed to comment, 'All [Tamburlaine's] raging cannot make her live'— just as it cannot prevent his own death. Instances of an increasing objectivity and critical detachment are undoubtedly there, in the play: it may be doubted however whether they do more than offer a temporary check to the underlying emotional drive.

[1] 'Hero and Leander', *Scrutiny*, II, 1, June 1933.

Miss Mahood says of Tamburlaine's death that it is 'the last in a series of events which have shown him that man cannot usurp power over life and death for his own ends'. Maybe; but to me the imaginative effect of the last Act cannot be reduced to that stark reality. Tamburlaine's savage cruelty towards the Governor and inhabitants of Babylon is perhaps commented on by the verse—'hesitating on the edge of caricature'—in which the mass drowning is described—

> fishes, fed by human carcasses,
> Amazed, swim up and down upon the waves—

as well as by Tamburlaine's sudden distemper. But the final scene opens with a long formal lament by the devoted followers —'Blush, heaven, to lose the honour of thy name' etc.—which is obviously intended to be taken seriously. And although in Tamburlaine's defiance of fate hyperbole is, it seems, deliberately deflated—

> Come let us march against the powers of heaven,
> And set black streamers in the firmament,
> To signify the slaughter of the gods.
> Ah, friends, what shall I do? I cannot stand.
> Come, carry me to war against the gods—

that is not the end. Tamburlaine is allowed to win one more effortless victory, to describe at length (with the aid of an impressive map) his career of conquest, and to make a noble departure from the scene.

> Meet heaven and earth, and here let all things end,
> For earth hath spent the pride of all her fruit,
> And heaven consum'd his choicest living fire!

It may be an exaggeration to say, as Kocher does, that 'all is sympathy, adoration and grief'; but what we find at the climax is surely alternation of attitude rather than any real growth of understanding.

iv

If I have spent what may seem a disproportionate amount of
time on *Tamburlaine* it is because that play gives us the clue to
Marlowe's failure ever to bring his gifts to fruition in a coherent 'criticism of life'—for 'criticism of life' is what the plays
are, in part, directed towards.[1] The material of the plays that
succeed *Tamburlaine* is the behaviour of men in sixteenth-
century England—their greed for power and money, their
violence, falsehood and (in the Elizabethan sense) 'policy', all
summed up in Machiavel's scornful prologue to *The Jew of
Malta*.

> Albeit the world think Machiavel is dead,
> Yet was his soul but flown beyond the Alps;
> And, now the Guise is dead, is come from France,
> To view this land, and frolic with his friends.
> To some perhaps my name is odious,
> But such as love me, guard me from their tongues,
> And let them know that I am Machiavel,
> And weigh not men, and therefore not men's words.
> Admir'd I am of those that hate me most:
> Though some speak openly against my books,
> Yet will they read me, and thereby attain
> To Peter's chair; and, when they cast me off,
> Are poison'd by my climbing followers.
> I count religion but a childish toy,
> And hold there is no sin but ignorance.
> Birds of the air will tell of murders past:

[1] It is understandable that A. P. Rossiter, comparing *Edward II* with
Woodstock, should speak of Marlowe's 'profound introversion': 'even in
seeming conflict', he says, 'the characters metaphorically stand back-to-
back and bawl and counterbawl about their own fates to the stars' (*Woodstock: a Moral History*, Preface, p. 65). But this refers to temperament
rather than to intention: my point is that the former stood in the way of the
latter.

I am asham'd to hear such fooleries.
Many will talk of title to a crown:
What right had Caesar to the empery?
Might first made kings, and laws were then most sure
When, like the Draco's, they were writ in blood. . . .

Marlowe's overt attitude towards this behaviour, and the
hypocrisy and stupidity that so often accompanied it, is one of
contempt; and to express his own peculiar blend of exasperation
and irony he develops a manner that, as T. S. Eliot noted long
ago, points forward to Ben Jonson. In the process he is impelled
to a radical questioning of what seem to have been his own
fundamental assumptions[1]—a labour of intelligence that shows
in the cutting-edge of some of his best verse. It may be doubted,
however, whether he ever succeeded in understanding, and so
mastering, his own fantasies. That, at all events, seems to me the
only explanation for the lapses and uncertainty of purpose that
prevent even his best work from being completely satisfying.
There are emotional entanglements at the roots of his conscious
attitudes, and he is too heavily committed to what his intelligence condemns.

Both *The Jew of Malta* and *The Tragical History of Dr Faustus*
demand full and serious attention; each, in different ways,
alternately rewards and frustrates the attention it demands. One
would need to be obstinately dull not to enjoy large stretches of
The Jew. Marlowe's sardonic intelligence is genuinely engaged
with what actually goes on in his world—a world where either
you eat or are eaten, and where unction is a sure sign of corrupt
purpose. When the rulers of Malta have swindled Barabas out of
all his possessions, it would be difficult to improve on the almost

---

[1] Levin says that '*Edward II* would prove, if it proved no more, Marlowe's
ability to challenge his own assumptions' (*The Overreacher*, p. 126), and
certainly there are many passages that show Marlowe being critical of
attitudes previously endorsed. But the insights are fragmentary; there is no
controlling 'idea'.

Dickensian command of speech inflexions through which the hypocrisy of the whole affair is exposed.

> *Barabas.* Will you, then, steal my goods?
> Is theft the ground of your religion?
> *Ferneze.* No, Jew; we take particularly thine,
> To save the ruin of a multitude:
> And better one want for a common good,
> Than many perish for a private man:
> Yet, Barabas, we will not banish thee,
> But here in Malta, where thou gott'st thy wealth,
> Live still; and, if thou canst, get more.
> *Barabas.* Christians, what, or how can I multiply?
> Of naught is nothing made.
> *First Knight.* From naught at first thou cam'st to little wealth,
> From little unto more, from more to most:
> If your first curse fall heavy on thy head,
> And make thee poor and scorn'd of all the world,
> 'Tis not our fault, but thy inherent sin.
> *Barabas.* What, bring you scripture to confirm your wrongs?
> Preach me not out of my possessions.
> Some Jews are wicked, as all Christians are;
> But say the tribe that I descended of
> Were all in general cast away for sin,
> Shall I be tried by their transgression?
> The man that dealeth righteously shall live:
> And which of you can charge me otherwise?
> *Ferneze.* Out, wretched Barabas!
> Sham'st thou not thus to justify theyself,
> As if we knew not thy profession?
> If thou rely upon thy righteousness,
> Be patient, and thy riches will increase.
> Excess of wealth is cause of covetousness:
> And covetousness, O, 'tis a monstrous sin!

Christians are hypocrites: this is the message of the action between Barabas and his adversaries.

Rather had I, a Jew, be hated thus,
Than pitied in a Christian poverty:
For I can see no fruits in all their faith,
But malice, falsehood, and excessive pride,
Which methinks fits not their profession.[1]

And if the Jew is a greedy monster he only embodies without disguise that 'desire of gold' which is 'the wind that bloweth all the world besides'. It is through a half-complicity with him that we see how wicked the world is.[2] But it is the nature of that complicity, and the uses to which Marlowe puts his central figure, that we find ourselves questioning. Great merchant, comic monster, master of policy, whining victim—these transformations we could perhaps assimilate if we felt that Marlowe, as deliberate artist, were sure of his tone—of his attitude towards his audience, and towards his subject. I for one cannot believe that he is; and a play that at times deserves the description of 'serious farce' at others becomes something like an undergraduate parody of a play that had yet to be written. The success, in short, is local and sporadic. I spoke earlier of the energies of art, and clearly, when the work is true, these spring not only from the immediate verbal organization but from the interaction of part with part, held steadily in one focus. In *The*

[1] In *2 Tamburlaine* (I, ii; II, i–iii) the Christian Sigismund is persuaded by his followers to break his solemn oath to Orcanes on the grounds that it is not necessary to keep faith with infidels.

[2] Part of the effect springs from the dramatist's zest in involving the audience in more than they had bargained for or quite knew they had got. When Machiavel, as Prologue, announces,

I come not, I,
To read a lecture here in Britain,

the implication is that since the lesson of 'policy' has already been learnt, the lecture is unnecessary. And when Barabas, engaged in his last and most monstrous deceit, turns directly to the audience—

Now tell me, worldlings, underneath the sun
If greater falsehood ever has bin done?

—it is just possible that some of the worldlings may have shaken their heads and murmured, 'never'. See Harry Levin, *The Overreacher*, pp. 93 ff.

Jew of Malta there is no focus; there is no unseen spectator—as there is, say, in *Volpone*—effectively disposing our attitudes to manipulator and victim alike. There are no standards, and by way of contempt alone there is no escape.

Is there—it now remains to ask—a way out in what must be regarded as Marlowe's greatest play? To what extent is *Dr Faustus* a product of the liberated imagination? To this question also there is no clear answer. Criticism, we know, should beware of interpreting particular works in the light of general notions imputed, on various grounds, to their author. *Dr Faustus* is important for what it is—a work of art in which the desire for effortless and unlimited power is subjected to the scrutiny of a powerful mind—and not merely as a document in the history of Marlowe's religious beliefs. In attempting a total estimate of the dramatist, however, it is impossible not to be puzzled by the relation between the orthodoxy so emphatically asserted in the play and the opinions attributed to Marlowe both by Kyd and Baines. And the fact that there *is* a puzzle may throw some light on the play itself.

Marlowe's persistent concern with religion was certainly not confined to exposing the gulf between the beliefs and the practices of professing Christians, and Kocher is right to insist on that fundamental aspect of Marlowe's thought. It is doubtful, however, whether he was the dedicated rationalist that Kocher makes him out to be. In the documents to which I have referred there are strictly rational arguments and objections to the fundamentalist strain in contemporary Christian thought, but there are also merely exasperated assertions of anti-Christian attitudes. And although the latter may be explained in part by the failure of his Christian contemporaries to meet him—as a Hooker could have met him—with more than dogmatic assertions, there is a residue of what seems like mere obsessive blasphemy. Referring to some of Marlowe's more outrageous statements, Kyd said, 'he would so suddenly take slight occasion to slip

[them] out'. 'Almost into every company he cometh,' said Baines, 'he persuades men to atheism.' In both statements there is the suggestion of a compulsive need; and although it would be useless and impertinent to try to trace this compulsion to its sources, it may nevertheless offer a clue to the ambivalent effect of *Dr Faustus*.

No one who studies the play with any care can subscribe to the view that Marlowe damns Faustus unwillingly, either as a concession to orthodoxy or because of a final failure of nerve. No one writes poetry of the order of Faustus's last terrible soliloquy without being wholly engaged,[1] and more than in any other of his plays Marlowe shows that he knows what he is doing. From the superbly presented disingenuousness of the opening soliloquy, in which Faustus dismisses the traditional sciences with a series of quibbles, Marlowe is making a sustained attempt to present as it really is the perverse and infantile desire for enormous power and immediate gratifications.

> O what a world of profit and delight,
> Of power, of honour and omnipotence,
> Is promis'd to the studious artizan!
> All things that move between the quiet poles
> Shall be at my command.[2]

[1] A point developed by James Smith in a notable essay, 'Marlowe's *Dr Faustus*' in *Scrutiny*, VIII, June 1939.

[2] If this is not sufficiently placed by the immediate context, there is the implicit comment in Faustus's words to Valdes and Cornelius (complete only in the A text) which editors have strangely found obscure:

> Know that your words have won me at the last
> To practise magic and concealed arts:
> Yet not your words only, but *mine own fantasy*,
> *That will receive no object*. . . .

Marlowe also slips in a hint or two that Faustus's prowess as a scholar had contained an element of self-inflation and aggression: his 'subtle syllogisms Gravell'd the pastors of the German church' etc. (I, i, 113 ff.); and one can almost hear the scholar's pride with which he 'was wont to make our schools ring with *sic probo*' (I, ii, 1-2).

However deeply Marlowe may have been versed in demonology it is unlikely that he took very seriously the business of 'Lines, circles, letters and characters'. Baudelaire says somewhere, '*Tout homme qui n'accepte pas les conditions de la vie vend son âme*'[1]; and a modern writer, James Baldwin, 'Everything in a life depends on how that life accepts its limits'.[2] It is in the light of such remarks that we should see the pact with the devil and the magic: they serve as dramatic representations of the desire to ignore that 'rightness of limitation', which, according to Whitehead, 'is essential for growth of reality'.[3] Marlowe—the overreacher—was only too familiar with that desire, and the turning on himself—on the self of *Tamburlaine*, Part I—is a measure of his genius.

Some such intention as I have described, the intention of coming to terms with a corrupting day-dream, determines the main structural lines and the great passages of *Dr Faustus*. But few even of the play's warmest admirers claim that it lives in the imagination as an entirely satisfying and consistent whole. Interest flags and is fitfully revived. And although the scenes in which Faustus's power is exhibited in such imbecile ways may be defended as presenting the gross stupidity of sin, this always feels to me, in the reading, as an explanation that has been thought up. With one or two exceptions, Faustus's capers represent an escape from seriousness and full realization—not simply on Faustus's part but on Marlowe's: and what they pad out is a crucial gap in the play's imaginative structure. For where, we may ask, are the contrasting positives against which Faustus's misdirection of his energies could be measured?

With this we return once more to the unresolved conflicts, the intrusive subjectivity, in terms of which it seems necessary to explain this remarkable play, as they are necessary to explain the obvious failures. It is not merely that—unlike Macbeth—

---

[1] Quoted by Enid Starkie, *Rimbaud*, p. 123.
[2] *Nobody Knows my Name: More Notes of a Native Son*, p. 145.
[3] A. N. Whitehead, *Religion in the Making* (Meridian Books), p. 146.

Faustus has no vision of the life-giving values against which he has offended: Marlowe doesn't grasp them either. And you have the uneasy feeling that Faustus's panic fear of hell is not only the inevitable result of a wilful, self-centred denial of life. It is as though Marlowe himself felt guilt about *any* of his assertive drives (understandably enough, since they were tied up with his regressions), and conceived of religion not in terms of a growth into freedom and reality but as binding and oppressing.

We may put this in another way. I have said that in some important respects Marlowe's creative fantasy did not meet sufficient resistance—the kind of resistance that is necessary for the production of the highest kind of energy, which is at once affirmation, growth and understanding. In *Dr Faustus* the resistance is, as it were, externalized. The anarchic impulse (the Ganymede-Tamburlaine fantasy) collides with a prohibition. Because what is prohibited and rebuked in this play is indeed a denial of life, and because the rebuke is charged with the full force of that other self of Marlowe's which appears so fitfully in the other plays, the result is poetry of very great power indeed. But even in the last great despairing speech, where almost over-powering feeling moulds the language in a way in which it had never been moulded before, the reader's submission is, I suggest, of a different order from the submission one gives to the greatest art, where a sense of freedom is the concomitant of acceptance of reality, however painful this may be.

If this is indeed so, it does something to explain how the orthodoxy of *Dr Faustus* and the animus against religion in the Baines document and elsewhere could be harboured simultaneously. It also helps to explain the diametrically opposed views to be found among the critics of the play. It seems to me that those who see the final soliloquy as the logical culmination of the play's action are right; and that those who see a more or less deliberate suppression of Marlowe's sympathy for his hero, in order to bring about an orthodox dénouement, are wrong. But the latter are in fact responding to an unresolved emotional quality that lies behind the rational structure of the play.

What we find in Marlowe's work therefore, besides great verbal power, is a critical intelligence almost, but not quite, of the first order, combined with unruly and conflicting emotions that were never fully clarified in a compelling dramatic image. But on this occasion it is proper for the critic—whose abilities are of a quite different order from those of the poet—to conclude by reflecting that Marlowe's great powers were at least struggling towards clarification. And he would be a foolhardy critic who, contemplating *Dr Faustus* and *The Jew of Malta*, would deny the quality of greatness in such diverse achievement.[1]

[1] In preparing this paper I was conscious of a special debt, for stimulus and suggestion (which did not always involve agreement), to the books and essays on Marlowe by J. A. Symonds, James Smith, Harry Levin, Paul Kocher, and M. M. Mahood, and to frequent conversations with Mr Wilbur Sanders.

The Social Background of Metaphysical Poetry

IT seems appropriate to begin a paper of this kind with the simple reminder that works of literature, once they have left their authors' hands, are only kept alive by being re-created and possessed by individuals, and that it is only in terms of their active re-creation in the fresh individual context of my experience and your experience that the main function of literature can be defined. In other words, literature is important because it *means* something to you and me and to everyone who is willing to accept its creative discipline; because it takes its place in the developing experience of our lives. It can, of course, serve other interests, such as the one I intend to pursue here—an interest in the meaning of 'culture' and in the relations of culture with economic and social activities; but it can only serve them at all fruitfully when they stem from that vivid personal apprehension and enjoyment that is the basis of all good criticism, as it is the main end of all reading.

It is in the light of these simple truths that we should consider T. S. Eliot's remark about 'sociological criticism, which has to suppress so much of the data, and which is ignorant of so much of the rest'.[1] The question is, What *are* the data of 'sociological criticism'? My own answer would be that the relevant evidence is of very varied kinds, but that the primary and indispensable evidence is that offered by literary criticism, by the co-ordinated sensitiveness, powers of analysis, tact, and sense of values of the individual playing upon literature itself. Divorced from *taste*, sociological criticism becomes the barren exercise it so often is. Taste alone will not of course provide all the evidence—the data— needed for an inquiry of this kind. But it is only a developed

[1] *The Use of Poetry and the Use of Criticism*, pp. 75–6.

feeling for literature, a responsiveness to the varied uses of language, that will tell us *what we are inquiring about*. When we have some idea of that we can usefully pursue our researches outside literature.

What we are inquiring is, in the first place, I suppose, to what extent the interests, perceptions, and modes of judgment, embodied in the fresh original creation of a work of art, are fostered and stabilized by day-to-day living in the society within which the artist works.[1] We want to know, therefore, something about such things as these: (i) The nature of the predominant forms of work—of getting a living—in any period, with special emphasis on the varied other-than-economic satisfactions involved; (ii) the forms of personal and wider social relations (beginning with the smaller units of family and neighbourhood), and the relations between different social groups; (iii) the traditions active in different groups and in the nation as a whole—religious, educational, 'cultural', and political traditions, traditions of personal behaviour and responsibility, and so on. We want to know a good many other things too, ranging from what may be called the practical organization of culture (the channels of demand and supply in literature and the other arts, and so on), to the current feeling for Nature and the natural processes. So the programme I have sketched is not one that can be carried out by any one person: it is essentially a matter for co-operative inquiry. But if we are agreed that the culture of a period depends on the kind and quality of the interests and modes of being fostered in ways such as I have indicated, and that these in turn are only present for discussion when the investigator has a sensitiveness to specific values similar in kind to that of the good critic, then we have some hope of making sociological criticism something other than

[1] I say 'to what extent' these are fostered in order not to seem to beg too many questions. An original artist may well, of course, reject much of the 'social' experience of his age; but that only means that the relationship is more complicated than when he speaks *for* his age; it is certainly not abolished. And no artist is completely 'original', or completely independent of his time.

an academic *substitute* for literary criticism, and of making it useful. If you ask me what the use is, I should say that, apart from strengthening our hold on literature that we like, it has the use of all historical and sociological study that is permeated by a sense of human values; that it deepens our insight into the intimate dependence of individual growth on factors outside the individual, and makes more vivid and specific the truth that civilization is essentially co-operative, involving co-operation with the living and the dead. In these ways it offers us principles that can guide our thinking about some of the more fundamental problems of the present. Since these are often distorted or obscured in the abstract terms of politics, sociological criticism (as I intend it) has the additional advantage of bringing us back from abstractions to the realities of personal satisfactions and personal fulfilment in certain specific circumstances.

After this beginning, what I actually have to offer will probably appear extremely slight. I shall be concerned with only a very few of the ways in which it is possible to work out *from* literature —from Metaphysical poetry—to 'the life of the time' in the early seventeenth century; and even within the narrow limits I have chosen I can only suggest what seem to me to be interesting possibilities. What follows is, then, little more than a draft programme of work to be done.

i

The observation to start from is that Metaphysical poetry touches life at many points. I am not referring to subject-matter (though that is varied), but to the range of interest and awareness that is brought to bear on any 'subject'. We come from the poetry with a renewed sense of the multiple nature of man, of the possibility—actualized in the best of the poems—of living simultaneously at many levels. In Donne's love poetry, for example, man—the actual experiencing individual—is felt as intimately enmeshed in the world of sense and instinct; and sense and passion are vividly expressed in their fresh immediacy. But in Donne there is always present the need to become *fully* aware of the immediate emotion, and the effort to apprehend—to grasp and realize—leads inevitably to the quickening of faculties so often only dimly present in the expression of sensation and feeling. In the best of his love poems there is active not only passion or affection but a ranging and inquiring mind and a spirit capable of perceiving values. Conversely, the most ecstatic experience is felt in terms 'which sense may reach and apprehend'. This is only another way of saying that in Donne thought, feeling and bodily sensation are intimately blended. And with this dimension of depth is a dimension of breadth: 'the most heterogeneous ideas' are brought to a focus. The range of Donne's intellectual and worldly interests is a commonplace of criticism; and it is because these interests are so vividly *there* —whether introduced directly or by way of simile and metaphor—that the greater poems of passion seem so solidly grounded.

> And though each spring do add to love new heat,
> As princes do in times of action get
> New taxes, and remit them not in peace,
> No winter shall abate the spring's increase.

The triumphant assurance of this—the conclusion of 'Love's Growth'—does not depend on any exclusion of the world of which the lovers form a part. Throughout *Songs and Sonets* the love themes are defined in terms of the poet's interest in an eager, active world of merchants and astronomers, princes and their favourites, schoolboys and prentices:

> Soldiers find wars, and lawyers find out still
> Litigious men, which quarrels move,
> Though she and I do love.

And besides the range of interests there is also a range of feeling.
Thus the love expressed in the greater poems, intensely personal
though it is, is not felt simply as an individual personal possession; it is felt in terms of more-than-personal life and growth:

> A single violet transplant,
> > The strength, the colour, and the size,
> (All which before was poor and scant,)
> > Redoubles still and multiplies.
> When love, with one another so
> > Interinanimates two souls . . .

> And yet no greater, but more eminent,
> > Love by the Spring is grown;
> > As in the firmament,
> Stars by the Sun are not enlarg'd, but shown.
> Gentle love deeds, as blossoms on a bough,
> From love's awakened root do bud out now.

These examples come from poems containing highly intellectual
argument, but they suggest that Donne shares something of the
feeling for *natural* growth—as wholesome and right for man—
that informs Shakespeare's plays:

> > For his bounty,
> There was no winter in it, an autumn 'twas
> That grew the more by reaping.

> She that herself will sliver and disbranch
> From her material sap, perforce must wither
> And come to deadly use.

Without overlooking the important differences from Donne,
we can say something similar of Herbert. Whereas Donne illuminates passion by play of mind, Herbert brings to the expression
of his religious experience the familiar world of everyday things.
But his homely imagery is not simply a form of expression; it is

an index of habitual modes of thought and feeling in which the different aspects and different levels of his personal experience are brought into intimate relation to each other. An additional observation is that the stream of his personal experience—more clearly than Donne's—is fed from sources apparently remote in the social topography of the period. His poetry, with its intellectual cast and its tone of courtesy, is plainly the work of one who moves easily in the cultivated circles of his time: 'I know the ways of learning ... honour ... pleasure'; and the contemporary learning that he assimilates takes its place in a solid traditional education that respects, without being overawed by, the new science. Thus scientific achievement and a certain complacence in the scientist are focused simultaneously in the first 'Vanity' poem.

> The fleet Astronomer can bore,
> And thread the spheres with his quick-piercing mind:
> He views their stations, walks from door to door,
> Surveys, *as if he had design'd*
> *To make a purchase there*: he sees their dances,
> And knoweth long before
> Both their full-ey'd aspects, and secret glances . . .

> The subtle Chymic can devest
> And strip the creature naked, till he find
> The callow principles within their nest:
> *There he imparts to them his mind*,
> Admitted to their bed-chamber, before
> They appear trim and drest
> To ordinary suitors at the door.

But if Herbert is courtly and Metaphysical he is also popular. He has an instinctive feeling for common speech—pithy, sententious, and shrewd, summing up character in a concrete image:

> Then came brave Glory puffing by
> In silks that whistled, who but he?

And as with Donne his interests and the modes of his sensibility are integrated in a uniquely personal idiom.[1]

What I am trying to do is to put into terms more immediately useful for my purpose the familiar conception of the Metaphysicals as possessing 'a mechanism of sensibility that could devour any kind of experience'. The later generation of these poets, apart from Marvell, had not the force of Donne or Herbert, but almost all the poets represented in Professor Grierson's well-known anthology express a vivid play of various interests that are felt as having an intimate bearing on each other: the sensibility is not compartmentalized. That is why the greater poems make such a disturbing, reverberating impact on the mind of the reader; even poems that appear slight on a first reading may be found to have behind them a range and weight of experience: there is 'the recognition, implicit in the expression of every experience, of other kinds of experience that are possible'.

Now the assumption on which I am working is that a positive distinctive quality common to half a dozen good poets and a number of competent and interesting ones, all writing within the same half-century, is not likely to be the result of a purely literary relationship to the founder of the 'school' whose individual genius can be regarded as the sole source of his followers' idiom. It is much more likely that the distinctive note of Metaphysical poetry—the implicit recognition of the many-sidedness of man's nature—is in some ways socially supported; that—to borrow some phrases from a suggestive passage in Yeats's criticism—'unity of being' has some relation to a certain 'unity of culture'. Professor Grierson remarks, 'It was only the force of Donne's personality that could achieve even an approximate harmony of elements so divergent as are united in his love-verses'.[2]

[1] For some discussion of Herbert relevant to the questions in hand I may refer to my essay on the poet in the earlier volume of *Explorations*.
[2] *The Poems of John Donne*, Vol. II, Introduction, p. lxvii.

When we recognize the truth in this, as we must, we need to keep in mind also the complementary truth tersely expressed by Ben Jonson: 'Rare poems ask rare friends'.[1]

ii

The tag from Jonson suggests where we should begin our inquiries. We need to know whom the Metaphysical poets expected to be interested in their verses, whom they met and at what levels, what were the functions, interests, and traditions of those who composed their immediate circle. All these questions represent work still to be done. We can say in a general way, however, that the social milieu of the Metaphysical poets was aristocratic in tone, connecting in one direction (partly but certainly not exclusively through patronage) with the inner circles of the Court, in another with the universities and with the middle and upper ranks of the ecclesiastical, administrative, and legal hierarchies, and in yet another with the prosperous merchant class represented by Izaak Walton and the Ferrars. A short study of the life of Sir Henry Wotton, a representative member of Donne's circle, may serve to point some provisional conclusions concerning the over-lapping aristocratic groups from which the 'rare friends' were drawn.

Henry Wotton was born in 1568. He came of a Kentish family that had provided the state with soldiers, administrators and diplomats throughout the Tudor period. Mr Logan Pearsall Smith, from whose admirable *Life* of Wotton I take my information,[2] tells us that, 'High public service, love of learning and of

---

[1] *To Lucy, Countess of Bedford, with M. Donne's Satires.*

[2] *The Life and Letters of Sir Henry Wotton,* 2 vols. (Oxford University Press). As well as the text, Appendix III, 'Notes on Sir Henry Wotton's Friends, Correspondents, and Associates', will be found useful by those who are interested in the interconnections of personal relationships in this period.

Italy and of poetry, were among the influences inherited from the past' (*Life and Letters*, I, p. 3). Educated at Winchester and Oxford, where he formed a lifelong friendship with John Donne, he went abroad to study law and languages. After five years in the German states, Austria, Italy, and Switzerland (where he spent fourteen months in the house of the scholar Casaubon) he returned to England and became one of the secretaries of the Earl of Essex. He accompanied Essex on the Cadiz expedition of 1596 and the Islands Voyage of 1597 (again in company with Donne), and on the disastrous Irish expedition of 1599. There followed a further adventurous period on the Continent, in which he was of service to the future James I, and early in the new reign he was knighted and sent as ambassador to the Venetian Republic. Wotton served three terms as ambassador in Venice, from 1604 to 1610, from 1616 to 1619, and again from 1621 to 1623. Between the first two of these he was engaged in various diplomatic missions, and he sat in the Addled Parliament of 1614. For a short period in 1612 he was in disgrace because of some unexpected consequences of his 'definition of an Ambassador': 'An Ambassador is an honest man sent to lie abroad for the good of his country'. Between the second and the third embassies to Venice Wotton was employed in James I's fruitless negotiations with the Emperor for a European peace. When he finally returned to settle in England in 1623 he was given the Provostship of Eton, and in 1626 he entered deacon's orders. At Eton, with occasional visits to London, Oxford, and his old home in Kent, he passed the tranquil remainder of his life, reading, writing, fishing, and taking a lively interest in the boys of the school. In 1638, the year before his death, he was visited by Milton, and in reply to a subsequent letter and a gift copy of *Comus* wrote his well-known commendation of that poem.

Robert Boyle, the famous chemist, who as a boy spent some time directly under Wotton's charge in the Provost's house at Eton, described him as 'a person that was not only a fine gentleman himself, but very well skilled in the art of making others so' (op. cit. I, p. 204). To consider Wotton's activities, interests and attainments is to form an idea of the qualities that the age considered proper to a fine gentleman. A large part of Wotton's adult life was spent in the service of the state, and he has of course a place in the political and diplomatic history of the time. But he was far from being merely a public figure. 'A wit and courtier, with the self-possession of a man of action, ready for any adventure and disguise, he was yet by nature and inclination a scholar and student; and beneath his cosmopolitan experience, and the taste and culture of Italy, he had preserved something of the simplicity and piety of the old Wottons, and an untouched devotion to the religion of his country' (op. cit. I, p. 27). A scholar and a friend of scholars, he 'was deeply read in history and moral philosophy and civil law'. He had the thorough grounding in Latin common to men of his class; he spoke Italian perfectly, and knew Greek, French, and German. As a minor poet he is still remembered for his poem on Elizabeth of Bohemia and the 'Character of a Happy Life', written during his period of disgrace in 1612. His prose writings include *The State of Christendom*,[1] a fragmentary *Survey of Education*, and *The Elements of Architecture*, which is said to show the Palladian taste that reached England towards the end of the reign of James I.[2] He was also— to borrow a word from the later seventeenth century, whose tastes he in some ways anticipated—something of a *virtuoso*. He had an amateur interest in the 'superior novelties' of science; he sent to King James a copy of Galileo's *Nuncius Sidereus* (1610),

[1] Mr Logan Pearsall Smith believes this contemporary survey to be Wotton's.
[2] A remark from this treatise is of some interest in connection with the history of taste. Pointed arches, says Wotton, 'both for the natural imbecility of the sharp angle itself, and likewise for their very uncomliness, ought to be exiled from judicious eyes, and left to their first inventors, the Gothes or Lumbards, amongst other reliques of that barbarous age' (quoted in *Life and Letters*, I, p. 196).

which describes the discoveries made through the newly in-
vented telescope—commenting that these would involve some
radical changes in judicial astrology; he visited Kepler in 1620
and described the latter's *camera obscura* in a letter to Bacon, re-
marking, 'I owe your lordship even by promise ... some trouble
this way; I mean by the commerce of philosophical experiments,
which surely, of all other, is the most ingenuous traffic' (*Life and
Letters*, II, p. 205). He liked to visit the glass factories near Venice,
and he collected and sent home from Italy cuttings of flowers
and fruit trees. He was also one of the first English connoisseurs
of Italian art (op. cit. I, pp. 59–60). His will may be cited here as
suggesting the variety of his interests. It mentions, besides books,
manuscripts, and Italian pictures: 'my great Loadstone; and a
piece of Amber of both kinds naturally united, and only differ-
ing in degree of concoction, which is thought somewhat rare';
'a piece of Crystal Sexangular (as they all grow) grasping divers
several things within it, which I bought among the Rhaetian
Alpes, in the very place where it grew'; 'my *Viol di Gamba*,
which hath been twice in Italy'; and 'my chest, or Cabinet of
Instruments and Engines of all kinds of uses: in the lower box
whereof, are some fit to be bequeathed to none but so entire an
honest man' as the legatee[1] (op. cit. I, pp. 215–19).

What emerges very clearly from Mr Logan Pearsall Smith's
biography is that Wotton's scholarly, artistic, and quasi-scientific
interests were by no means private hobbies, carefully kept apart
from his public interests; they were shared with a large and
varied circle of friends, and they entered into his ordinary social
living. Mr Smith describes Wotton's habitual mode of life at
Venice:

> Being prohibited by his position from any association with the
> nobles of Venice, he was largely dependent for society on the

[1] According to Walton these were 'Italian Locks, Picklocks, Screws to
force open doors, and many other things of worth and rarity, that he had
gathered in his foreign Travel'.

members of his own household. But these young men, his own nephews, sons of Kentish squires, or scholars fresh from Oxford or Cambridge, formed just the kind of society in which he delighted.[1] Together they made what Wotton called a 'domestic college' of young Englishmen in their Venetian palace. They had their chaplain and their religious services; they read aloud the classics, or some new book of weight at stated hours,[2] and dined together, toasting by name their friends in England. They occupied themselves sometimes with music (the ambassador himself playing on the viol di gamba), sometimes with chemical experiments, or again with philosophical speculations, attempting, as Wotton put it, to mend the world in the speculative part, since they despaired of putting it right in the practical and moral . . . 'In summa we live happily, merrily, and honestly', one of his household writes; 'let State businesses go as they will, we follow our studies hard and love one another' (op. cit. I, pp. 57–8).

We do not really know how far upwards in the social scale the kinds of interest that we find in Wotton permeated. James I was bookish, and Charles I was a cultivated man, but it is quite likely that the tone of the inner court circle was set by men whose interests in the arts did not go very far beyond the opportunities for display that they afforded. The fact remains, however, that Wotton's circle was on a comparatively intimate footing with the greater social figures, and that it formed an integral part of the contemporary aristocracy.

[1] They included Nathaniel Fletcher, a brother of John Fletcher the dramatist, and Rowland Woodward, to whom some of Donne's verse letters are addressed.

[2] In 1620 Wotton wrote to thank Bacon for a gift copy of the *Novum Organum*. 'But of your said work (which came but this week to my hand)', he said, 'I shall find occasion to speak more hereafter; having yet read only the first book thereof, and a few aphorisms of the second. For it is not a banquet that men may superficially taste, and put up the rest in their pockets, but in truth a solid feast, which requireth due mastication. Therefore when I have once myself pursued the whole, I determine to have it read piece by piece at certain hours in my domestic college, as an ancient author' (op. cit. II, p. 204).

In so far as Wotton was representative of a class—and he was certainly not unrepresentative—two points of some importance for our understanding of the seventeenth century emerge. The first is that the aristocracy from whom so many of the friends and patrons of the Metaphysical poets were drawn was a functional aristocracy. The general significance of this was indicated by D. W. Harding in two articles in the *Musical Times* (May and June, 1938) on 'The Social Background of Taste in Music'.

Common experience suggests that the people who really influence public taste (at the moment chiefly by sanctioning its low level) are those who remain in close touch with industry and commerce and public affairs—what may conveniently be called the upper business class. The leisured are of less account. They or their ancestors were influential while they made their money, but once elevated to the ranks of the leisured they receive deference without possessing influence. They are respected for having secured their translation from the real world, but what they choose to do after metamorphosis is of no moment to those in 'active' life. The ideals which make some mark on general opinion are those of men like Lord Nuffield, who, besides being public-spirited, are also responsible industrialists, still in direct touch with business. And at present men of this sort may encourage public interest in the welfare of the unemployed or the usefulness of universities to business life, but they rarely stand effectively committed to a belief in the value of the arts.

Presumably (though here the evidence of the historian is required) the older traditions of respecting significant music grew up when the patrons of the arts were people of 'practical' importance—rulers, statesmen, ambassadors, men of power in the Church, merchant princes, lords in direct control of their estates. And their taste for music and the other arts was not an idiosyncrasy to be shut away in their private lives: it was an integral part of their public personality. To have had business dealings with them while remaining a confessed philistine must have been like meeting modern business men without knowing anything of golf courses, restaurants, the motor show, air travel, or foreign resorts; possible no doubt, but a trifle embarrassing on both sides.

The second point, which has a more direct bearing on the particular qualities of Metaphysical poetry, is that in this milieu there was not only 'a current of ideas', but a current fed from varied sources. Consider for a moment Ben Jonson. Jonson wrote masques for the Court and lyric poems that helped to set the tone of much court poetry in Charles's reign. He was a scholar, moving easily in the circle of ideas represented by such men as Camden, Casaubon and Selden. He was also a writer for the popular stage, with an eager interest in the everyday life of London and an ingrained feeling for that native vigour expressed in the colloquial English of his day. Wherever we look we find that the channels of interest form a criss-cross pattern. In Jonson's or Donne's or Wotton's circle, politics and public affairs, scholarship and 'the new philosophy', literature and the arts, meet and cross: they are not compartmentalized. In other words, the milieu offers a variety of interests; it offers a positive incentive to flexibility of mind, and so does something to prepare the ground for that maturity of judgment that comes when varied fields of experience are seen in relation to each other.

In another way too Wotton can be instanced as representative. 'Izaak Walton rightly insists', says Mr Logan Pearsall Smith, 'on the importance of Bocton [the family home in Kent] in the history of Sir Henry Wotton's life. It was indeed the memories and traditions centred about this ancient house that played a predominant part in the formation of his character. From his family and ancestors he inherited that peculiar combination of culture and old-fashioned piety, of worldly wisdom and ingenuousness of nature, "the simplicity", as he called it, "of a plain Kentish man", which gave in after years a certain graceful singularity to his conduct, difficult for the courtiers among whom he moved to understand. He loved everything that savoured of Kent, all the local ways and phrases, and when

ambassador abroad he surrounded himself with the sons of
Kentish neighbours. Bocton he always regarded as his home,
finding even the air about it better and more wholesome than
other air; to the end of his life he returned thither when he could,
although as a younger son he possessed no claim on the place save
that of affection' (*Life and Letters*, I, pp. 3-4). I am very doubtful
of Wotton's 'singularity' in this respect. At all events the country
house in this period had an importance not merely social but
cultural. Few of the greater places can have maintained such a
vigorous intellectual life as contemporaries admired at Tew,
where Lucius Cary, Viscount Falkland, gathered his friends and
made what Clarendon called 'a University bound in a lesser
volume'.[1] But the tradition of 'housekeeping' inherited by a
good many noblemen and gentlemen of the early seventeenth
century seems to have included the duty of maintaining, in
various capacities and for longer or shorter periods, scholars and
men of letters. And because the great houses were an integral
part of English rural life—not just holiday resorts for hunting
and shooting—their owners were genuinely in touch with the
activities and traditions of the countryside. Ben Jonson was a
shrewd and realistic observer of the life about him, and this is
how he described Penshurst, the seat of the Sidney family in
Kent.[2]

> The blushing apricot and woolly peach
> Hang on thy walls, that every child may reach.
> And though thy walls be of the country stone,
> They are reared with no man's ruin, no man's groan;
> There's none that dwell about them wish them down,
> But all come in, the farmer and the clown,
> And no one empty handed, to salute

[1] See the extracts from Clarendon's account of Falkland in D. Nichol
Smith's *Characters from the Histories and Memoirs of the Seventeenth Century*,
pp. 71 ff. and p. 169.
[2] Owned at the time Jonson wrote of it by Sir Robert Sidney, Viscount
Lisle, the younger brother of Sir Philip Sidney.

Thy lord and lady, though they have no suit.
Some bring a capon, some a rural cake,
Some nuts, some apples; some that think they make
The better cheeses bring 'em, or else send
By their ripe daughters whom they would commend
This way to husbands, and whose baskets bear
An emblem of themselves in plum or pear . . .

This is an idealized but not, I think, a misleading picture, and it gives a fair impression of what 'housekeeping' meant for many great families of the time. It meant hospitality, and it meant sharing in the community life of the village in a fairly intimate fashion. It meant something altogether different from a condescending interest in 'the villagers'. In the same poem Jonson tells how King James paid a surprise visit to Penshurst when the mistress of the house was away:

What great I will not say, but sudden cheer
Didst thou then make 'em! and what praise was heaped
On thy good lady then! who therein reaped
The just reward of her high huswifery;
To have her linen, plate, and all things nigh
When she was far, and not a room but dressed
As if it had expected such a guest.

The 'good lady' who is praised for her 'high huswifery' is Lady Lisle, and it is significant that Jonson can use these homely terms in her praise.[1]

[1] We are reminded of the description of a sixteenth-century Lady Berkeley, given by John Smyth towards the end of the reign of James I: 'Country huswifery seemed to be an essential part of this lady's constitution; a lady that . . . would betimes in winter and summer mornings make her walks to visit her stable, barns, day-house, poultry, swinetroughs and the like; which huswifery her daughter-in-law . . . seeming to decline, and to betake herself to the delights of youth and greatness, she would sometimes to those about her swear, By God's blessed sacrament, this gay girl will beggar my son Henry' (*The Berkeley Manuscripts*, II, p. 254). See also George Herbert's description of the activities of his mother, Mrs Magdalen Herbert, included in Edmund Blunden's translation of the Latin verses, *Memoriae Matris Sacrum—Essays and Studies of the English Association*, xix, 1933.

I do not want to idealize the life of the aristocratic households in town and country in which the poets and men of letters had a footing. But it does seem true to say that they were places where a variety of living interests were taken for granted, and where men of different bents and occupations could find some common ground.[1] And since the country houses were still functional units in the rural economy of the time,[2] I think they helped to foster that intimate feeling for natural growth and the natural order—something so very different from the modern 'appreciation of nature'—that almost disappears from English poetry after Marvell.[3]

iii

The question of the traditions active in the social groups from which the Metaphysical poets were drawn is far too large for me to venture on any inclusive generalizations. I will only note one or two features of the religious tradition that have a direct bearing on my present theme.

[1] It is significant that, according to Walton, when Donne was in the service of Ellesmere, the Lord Chancellor, the latter 'esteemed his company and discourse to be a great ornament' to his own table.

[2] See the early pages of the *Memoirs of the Verney Family during the Seventeenth Century*. In my *Drama and Society in the Age of Jonson*, pp. 111-17, I have listed some of the contemporary complaints of the decay of 'housekeeping', which suggest what was still considered its proper function.

[3] Since this was written the matter has been much more fully considered by G. R. Hibbard in an article on 'The Country House Poem of the Seventeenth Century' (*Journal of the Warburg and Courtauld Institutes*, Vol. XIX, Nos. 1-2, 1956). Mr Hibbard writes: 'From the middle of the seventeenth century the poet became less dependent on the patron; and, while the country house became grander than before, and even continued as a cultural centre for another century, it no longer occupied that focal position in the life of the nation which it had held during the first half of the seventeenth century.'

We have recently been reminded that Donne and his generation were the inheritors of the medieval view of man that saw
him as half way between the beasts and the angels, and as sharing
something of the nature of both. According to this view man
shares sense and instinct with the animals. Like the angels, he
is capable of intellectual knowledge, but whereas the angels
know at once, intuitively, man can only attain knowledge of a
limited kind by the exercise of reason. Wretched and worth-
less through sin, he is capable of salvation through grace. The
medieval view of man's central place in the universe was undermined by the discoveries and new intellectual currents of the
Renaissance. Donne and his contemporaries were forced to
question the old assumptions: 'The new philosophy puts all in
doubt'. But all the same they were still conscious of the old
tradition which sanctioned the view of man as a being existing
at many levels—not just a rational being as the eighteenth
century tended to see him, not just an economic unit as a powerful trend of thought in the nineteenth century was content to
assume. Now 'the idea of man' implicit or explicit in the religious tradition has its own importance. But there is something
more important, though more difficult to formulate: I mean the
fact that religion in the early seventeenth century is not set over
against life; it still in some way *grows out of* the life that it sets
itself to foster. George Herbert is close enough to the central Anglican tradition to be instanced as representative. That
Herbert's religion is not lacking in elements of imaginative
grandeur may be seen from the powerful dramatic poem,
'The Sacrifice', and no one who knows his poems of
personal exploration and self-discovery will think of him in
terms of a naïve piety. But to understand Herbert we need to
know not only his greater poems—poems that appeal to men of
very different faiths—but also his more pedestrian verses where
he states very simply the bases of his faith and outlook. There is,
for example, 'The Church-Porch', where the precepts of good

neighbourliness are tempered and refined by Herbert's personal courtesy and feeling for other people as individuals. And behind this feeling for the direct contact of men in small social units is a pervasive sense of the wider order of nature in which the parish or neighbourhood has its setting and to which it belongs. We see something of this in 'Providence':

> Sheep eat the grass, and dung the ground for more:
> Trees after bearing drop their leaves for soil.

It is the fact that Herbert does not need to insist (for the assumption is that everybody knows) that makes this significant. It is not an accident that in the greater poems of personal experience—in 'Vertue', 'Life' and 'The Flower', for example—the defining is done in terms of imagery drawn from the world of seasonal growth, decay and renewal. The bearing of this aspect of the religious tradition is clear when we consider the implications of the very different idiom of the later seventeenth century. There is no need to question the sincerity of Dryden's religious beliefs, either in *Religio Laici* or *The Hind and the Panther*; but those beliefs—except when they draw on Dryden's powerful conception of social order—seem to have very little to do with his most vital mundane interests.

> Rest then, my soul, from endless anguish freed:
> Nor sciences thy guide, nor sense thy creed.
> Faith is the best insurer of thy bliss;
> The bank above must fail before the venture miss.[1]

A religion that can be expressed in such terms has plainly lost connexion with the deeper sources of vitality and spiritual health; and for this reason it cannot enrich human living with a sense of significance in all its parts, as the tradition active in Herbert's— and in Shakespeare's—day enriched it.

[1] *The Hind and the Panther*, Part I, ll. 146–9.

iv

The conditions I have described could not last. In Carew's
poem, *In Answer of an Elegiacal Letter, upon the Death of the King
of Sweden* . . . (1632), the poet praises the 'halycon days' of
Charles I.

> But let us, that in myrtle bowers sit
> Under secure shades, use the benefit
> Of peace and plenty, which the blessed hand
> Of our good king gives this obdurate land;
> Let us of revels sing . . .
> . . . What though the German drum
> Bellow for freedom and revenge, the noise
> Concerns not us, nor should divert our joys;
> Nor ought the thunder of their carabines
> Drown the sweet airs of our tuned violins.

Even here there is a suggestion of a culture self-conscious and on
the defensive. In Marvell the older tradition is still active. But
Marvell's greatest poem is concerned with the clash of irreconcilable forces long latent in society.

> Though Justice against Fate complain,
> And plead the ancient Rights in vain:
> But those do hold or break
> As Men are strong or weak.
> Nature that hateth emptiness,
> Allows of penetration less:
> And therefore must make room
> Where greater Spirits come.

A glance at the background of literature in the period immediately following the mid-century break may serve to bring
out by contrast what is meant by saying that Metaphysical
poetry touches life at many points, and that its implicit recognition of the many-sidedness of man's nature was socially sup-

ported. To start with, of course, the medieval traditions—questioned and undermined but still active in Donne's day—do not survive the Civil War. The new intellectual current is rationalist and materialist, pointing forward to the Enlightenment of the eighteenth century. Restoration assumptions concerning man's nature are narrower than those previously accepted. Whereas man had been recognized as a complex being, rooted in instinct, swayed by passions, and at the same time an intellectual and spiritual being, he is now something much simpler. He is a reasonable creature, in the limited way in which the new age understood 'Reason': he is in fact something much more like a mechanism than a mystery; for, says Hobbes, 'What is the Heart, but a Spring; and the Nerves, but so many Strings; and the Joints but so many Wheels, giving motion to the whole Body, such as was intended by the Artificer?'[1] Partly in consequence of these changes in the intellectual climate literature tends to stress the rational and social elements in man to the exclusion of other qualities. Dryden is a great poet, but, as I have already suggested, there are wide ranges of human potentiality and human experience that he is quite unaware of.

The changes in social organization were equally marked. At the Restoration the Court was the centre of polite letters. But Charles II's courtiers, though some of them were interested in the Royal Society, were far from being the intellectual centre of a national culture. Wotton would have been sadly out of place at that Court, not only on account of his piety. Cultivated women such as the Countess of Bedford or Mrs Herbert disappear from the social scene. Country housekeeping in the old sense—though still a factor in the national life—is rapidly giving way before the attractions of a life in town. And what 'the Town' thought of the country is amply demonstrated in the comedies of

---

[1] *Leviathian*, The Introduction (Everyman edition), p. 1. The naked mechanistic attitude was of course qualified in the common acceptance; but that does not destroy Hobbes's representative significance.

the period. When one reads Professor Pinto's *Life* of Rochester, the most gifted of the mob of gentlemen who wrote with ease, one is conscious of a rather chilly wind of emptiness. It is symptomatic that in Rochester, 'wit', canalized into satire, is completely divorced from 'feeling'. And in the best of his love poems the feeling is both simple—a momentary tenderness— and quite unrelated to that fuller life so actively present in Donne's poems even when he is most absorbed by his passion.

Those aspects of the background of poetry in the early Stuart period that I have indicated need to be explored in detail before we can reach any certain conclusions about the influence of social life on poetry. And a fuller exploration would certainly make distinctions where I have generalized. (One obvious distinction would be between the first two decades of the seventeenth century, still partly Elizabethan, and the two or three decades that followed, when taste was certainly changing.'[1] But it does seem to me that further knowledge of the facts of social life in the first half of the seventeenth century is likely to substantiate the conclusions to which literary criticism points. They are: (i) that the social milieu of the Metaphysical poets was one in which there was an *active* culture: there was 'a current of ideas in the highest degree animating and nourishing to the creative power'; (ii) that through this milieu the poets whose work brings so much of the 'the whole soul of man into activity' touched life at many points. Tradition and the actual social organization alike fostered a range of contacts with contemporary life that is, to say the least, rare in the later history of English poetry.

[1] David Mathew's *The Jacobean Age* notes some of the shifting currents of taste in the wider social context up to Buckingham's assassination in 1628.

Reflections on Clarendon's
History of the Rebellion

THE title of my paper is intended to indicate both the un-
systematic and the non-specialized nature of my approach
to my subject. Clarendon is a great historian, and adequately to
assess his work as an historian demands qualifications that I
certainly do not possess. But the *History of the Rebellion* is not
merely a book for the specialist. It can be read with profit by all
who are interested in our civilization, its past and present. It
reveals a phase in that civilization. And when we reflect on what
it reveals we find that we are contemplating themes concerning
the relation of 'politics' and 'culture' that are of great importance.

It will soon be apparent that I admire Clarendon. So I had
better make plain at the start that I am aware of his limitations,
as no one with the slightest knowledge of the period can fail to
be. He certainly does not give us a complete picture of the Civil
War and its causes. He was a constitutional royalist, a church-
man, and a lawyer, with a great respect for precedent. He was
critical of the personal administration of Charles I, and severely
critical of his court. He approved of much of the legislation of the
first session of the Long Parliament, that limited the arbitrary
power of the Crown. He was a severe judge of the unruly faction
and self-seeking that contributed so largely to the failure of the
royal cause. But we look in vain in the *History* for any recognition of the deeper motives that united large masses of men in
fundamental opposition to king and bishop. He was completely
unaware of the widespread shift in economic power that gave
significance to the parliamentary slogan, 'Property and liberty'.
He had no understanding of the sober strength of Puritanism: he
saw only its fanatical and intolerant side. He can describe the
'discipline diligence and sobriety' of the parliamentary armies or

the spontaneous opposition of common people to the royalist armies in different parts of the country, and yet show no sign of recognizing that these are matters requiring some explanation. We may agree that the rebellion was directed by a very small number of men—'the great managers', as he calls them—but it could not have been in any degree successful without mass support. It was not *simply* brought about—as Clarendon often implies—by a handful of men 'who had the skill and cunning out of froward and ambitious humours and indispositions to compound fears and jealousies'. Much less was it merely—as Clarendon in one place calls it—a 'strange wild fire among the people'.

If, in spite of these limitations, the *History of the Rebellion* is one of the great books of the seventeenth century, it is because of certain qualities of mind that Clarendon brought to his task. These qualities of mind, implicit in Clarendon's handling of his material, form the starting-point of my reflections.

It is by his character-sketches—essays in a favourite seventeenth-century genre—that he is best known, and they are justly famous. 'Each of them', says Sir James Stephen, 'shows how closely and with what searching curiosity he examined and revolved in his mind any fact which interested him. Everyone, his dearest friend, his bitterest enemy, the objects of his deepest contempt and of his highest admiration, are all passed through the same crucible. He looks into them with all the curiosity of a modern novelist'.[1] And Professor Nichol Smith: 'All his characters are clearly defined. We never confound them; we never have any doubt of how he understood them. He sees men as a whole before he begins to describe them. . . . He does not build up his characters. He does not, as many others do, start with the external features in the hope of arriving at the central facts. He starts from the centre and works outwards. This is the reason of

[1] *Horae Sabbaticae*, First Series, p. 314.

the convincingness of his characters, their dramatic truth'.[1] What interests Clarendon is the essential bent of a man's mind, the motives that, ingrained in character, issue in significant action. He does not simplify. He has a special relish in revealing inconsistencies and in reconciling them. Each of his characters is judged; there is an explicit or implicit moral evaluation. The judgment is not always, we may feel, a fair one; but it is always based on Clarendon's own sense of the person. It is not—or not as a rule—imposed; it issues from a cultivated awareness in which moral taste and psychological acumen are combined.

For my purpose it is important that you should have before you some examples of the analytic power of which I have spoken. I have chosen two short sketches and two extracts from longer studies, that will illustrate Clarendon's skill in handling diverse material. The first is Attorney-General Noy:

> The first, upon the great fame of his ability and learning (and very able and learned he was), was by great industry and importunity from Court persuaded to accept that place for which all other men laboured ... and so he suffered himself to be made the King's Attorney-General. The Court made no impression upon his manners; upon his mind it did: and though he wore about him an affected morosity which made him unapt to flatter other men, yet even that morosity and pride rendered him the most liable to be grossly flattered himself that can be imagined. And by this means the great persons who steered the public affairs, by admiring his parts and extolling his judgment as well to his face as behind his back, wrought upon him by degrees, for the eminency of the service, to be an instrument in all their designs; thinking that he could not give a clearer testimony that his knowledge in the law was greater than all other men's, than by making that law which all other men believed not to be so. So he moulded, framed, and pursued the odious and crying pro-

[1] *Characters from the Histories and Memoirs of the Seventeenth Century*, 'Essay on the Character', p. 13.

ject of soap, and with his own hand drew and prepared the writ for ship-money, both of which will be the lasting monuments of his fame. In a word, he was an unanswerable instance how necessary a good education and knowledge of men is to make a wise man, at least a man fit for business. (I, 157)[1]

Beside this we may put the portrait of another honest man who also, in Clarendon's view, lacked certain necessary qualities of self-knowledge. Of the parliamentary general, the Earl of Essex, he writes:

. . . it shall suffice in this place to say, that a weak judgment, and a little vanity, and as much of pride, will hurry a man into as unwarrantable and as violent attempts as the greatest and most unlimited and insatiable ambition will do. He had no ambition of title, or office, or preferment, but only to be kindly spoken to, and quietly to enjoy his own fortune: and, without doubt, no man in his nature more abhorred rebellion than he did, nor could he have been led into it by any open or transparent temptation, but by a thousand disguises and cozenages. His pride supplied his want of ambition, and he was angry to see any other man more respected than himself, because he thought he deserved it more, and did better requite it. For he was in his friendships just and constant, and would not have practised foully against those he took to be enemies. No man had credit enough with him to corrupt him in point of loyalty to the King whilst he thought himself wise enough to know what treason was. But the new doctrine and distinction of allegiance, and of the King's power in and out of Parliament, and the new notions of ordinances, were too hard for him, and did really intoxicate his understanding, and made him quit his own to follow theirs who he thought wished as well and judged better than himself. His vanity disposed him to be *His Excellence*, and his weakness to believe that he should be general in the Houses as well as in the field, and be able

[1] References are to the book and paragraph of the *History* in Macray's edition (Oxford University Press).

to govern their counsels and restrain their passions as well as to fight their battles; and that by this means he should become the preserver, and not the destroyer, of the King and kingdom. And with this ill-grounded confidence he launched out into that sea where he met with nothing but rocks and shelves, and from whence he could never discover any safe port to harbour in. (VI, 402)

That may not be the actual Essex, but it is a portrait of someone who certainly might have existed. The picture of Laud exhibits a quite different blend of flaws and virtues. The main lines of his character are given in a few sentences:

He was a man of great courage and resolution, and being most assured within himself that he proposed no end in all his actions or designs than what was pious and just (as sure no man had ever a heart more entire to the King, the Church, or his country), he never studied the best ways to those ends; he thought, it may be, that any art or industry that way would discredit, at least make the integrity of the end suspected. Let the cause be what it will, he did court persons too little; nor cared to make his designs and purposes appear as candid as they were by shewing them in any other dress than their own natural beauty and roughness. (I, 196)

My last example—part of the study of Lord Digby—offers a marked contrast to the stubborn integrity of Laud.

He was a man of very extraordinary parts by nature and art, and had surely as good and excellent an education as any man of that age in any country: a graceful and beautiful person; of great eloquence and becomingness in his discourse (save that sometimes he seemed a little affected), and of so universal a knowledge that he never wanted subject for a discourse: he was equal to a very good part in the greatest affair, but the unfittest man alive to conduct it, having an ambition and vanity superior to all his

other parts, and a confidence peculiar to himself, which sometimes intoxicated and transported him. . . .

He had been instrumental in promoting the three persons
above mentioned [Hyde, Culpepper and Falkland] to the King's
favour, and had himself, in truth, so great an esteem of them that
he did very frequently, upon conference together, depart from his
own inclinations and opinions and concurred in theirs; and very
few men of so great parts are upon all occasions, more counsel-
lable than he; so that he would seldom be in danger of running
into great errors if he would communicate and expose all his own
thoughts and inclinations to such a disquisition; nor is he unin-
clinable in his nature to such an entire communication in all things
which he conceives to be difficult. But his fatal infirmity is that he
too often thinks difficult things very easy; and doth not consider
possible consequences when the proposition administers somewhat
that is delightful to his fancy, and by pursuing whereof he imag-
ines he shall reap some glory to himself, of which he is im-
moderately ambitious; so that, if the consultation be upon any
action to be done, no man more implicitly enters into that debate,
or more cheerfully resigns his own conceptions to a joint deter-
mination: but when it is once affirmatively resolved (besides that
he may possibly reserve some impertinent circumstance, as he
thinks, the imparting whereof would change the nature of the
thing), if his fancy suggests to him any particular which himself might perform in that action, upon the imagination that
everybody would approve it if it were proposed to them, he
chooses rather to do it than to communicate, that he may have
some signal part to himself in the transaction in which no other
person can claim a share. And by this unhappy temper he
did often involve himself in very unprosperous attempts. (IV,
127, 128)

To which may be added a sentence from a later volume (Digby,
defeated in battle, is about to retire to Ireland):

And the temper and composition of his mind was so admirable,
that he was always more pleased and delighted that he had ad-

vanced so far, which he imputed to his virtue and conduct, than broken or dejected that his success was not answerable, which he still charged upon second causes, for which he could not be accountable. (IX, 126)[1]

'Characters' such as these can be read with pleasure in isolation, but they lose something by being detached from their context and from each other. Some of them are set pieces, but the kind of interest they represent is pervasive throughout the *History*. There are frequent observations made in passing that show the student of human nature.

> Upon these and other motives, besides the natural credulity in men, in believing all they wished to be true, the King was prevailed with. . . .
> . . . revenge, which is a guest that naturally disquiets and tortures those who entertain it with all the perplexities they contrive for others.
> Mr Jermin, who still valued himself upon the impossible faculty to please all and displease none. . . .
> Mr L'Estrange spake to them in a style very much his own, and being not very clear to be understood, the more prevailed over them.
> He so far prevailed with his Highness, who would have been more choleric if he had had less right on his side. . . .

It is part of Clarendon's success that, by displaying events in a context of pondered personal comment, he can make us feel the complex pressure of the actual.

The characters, then, are integral to the *History* as a whole,

---

[1] Cf. also X, 13: 'He was a person of so rare a composition by nature and by art (for nature alone could never have reached to it), that he was so far from being ever dismayed upon any misfortune (and greater variety of misfortunes never befell any man), that he quickly recollected himself so vigorously, that he did really believe his condition to be improved by that ill accident, and that he had an opportunity thereby to gain a new stock of reputation and honour.'

and when we have understood the relation between Clarendon's attitude to persons and his attitude to events we may begin to understand the nature of that wisdom that makes the *History of the Rebellion* so much more than a source book for the period. What is it, we may ask, that gives so many of Clarendon's utterances on politics that weight which—whether or not we agree with his general position—we must allow them? It is partly, of course, the actual experience of affairs. Clarendon knows from direct observation how men behave in politics. When he speaks of 'that fathomless abyss of Reason of State', or when he says of a certain Earl ('much addicted to the mathematics') that 'he was in truth rather a speculative than a practical man, and expected a greater certitude in the consultation of business than the business of this world is capable of ', or when he remarks that 'the nature of men, especially of men in authority, is inclined rather to commit two errors than to retract one', we know that he is speaking out of his own experience. But it is not merely that Clarendon the historian possesses the acumen of Clarendon the statesman. There is a passage in Book VII concerning the utility of general councils that may illustrate my meaning.

And I cannot but on this occasion continue this digression thus much farther, to observe, that they who avoid public debates in Council, or think them of less moment, upon the undervaluing the persons of the councillors, and from the particular infirmities of men, the heaviness of this man, the levity of that, the weakness and simplicity of a third, conclude that their advice and opinions are not requisite to any great design, are exceedingly deceived, and will perniciously deceive others who are misled by those conclusions. For it is in wisdom as it is in beauty. A face that, being taken in pieces, affords scarce one exact feature, an eye, or a nose, or a tooth, or a brow, or a mouth, against which a visible just exception cannot be taken, yet altogether, by a gracefulness and vivacity in the whole, may constitute an excellent beauty, and be more catching than another whose symmetry is more faultless. So there are many men, who in this particular argument may be unskilful, in that affected, who may seem to have levity, or vanity, or formality, in ordinary cursory conversation (a very crooked rule to measure men's abilities, and gives a better evidence of the nature than of the understanding), and yet in formed counsels, deliberations, and transactions, are men of great insight and wisdom, and from whom excellent assistance is contributed.

And, no question, all great enterprises and designs that are to be executed have many parts, even in the projection, fit for the survey and disquisition of several faculties and abilities, and equally for the decision of sharper and more phlegmatic understandings. And we often hear in debates of great moment animadversions of more weight and consequence from those whose ordinary conversation is not so delightful, than from men of more sublime parts. Certainly Solomon very well understood himself when he said, '*In the multitude of counsellors there is safety*'. And though it were confessed that reason would be better stated and discovered, and conclusions easier made, by a few than a greater number, yet when the execution depends on many, and the general interpretation so much depends on the success, and the success on the interpretation, we see those counsels most prosperous whereof the considerations and deliberations have been measured by that standard which is most publicly received and acknowledged. (VII, 280–281)

Here, we may say, is political wisdom springing from a lifetime of political experience. True; but my point is that it is more than *political* wisdom. From the theory of general councils Clarendon turns to the actual divisions within the King's court at Oxford, to the faction, envy and egotism that prevented the emergence of a common will. In these circumstances, he said, it was very hard for a minister, exposed to envy on all sides, to achieve the necessary 'patience, temper and dexterity'; and he continues:

The best provision that such men can make for their voyage, besides a stock of innocence that cannot be impaired, and a firm confidence in God Almighty that he will never suffer that innocence to be utterly oppressed or notoriously defamed, is, an expectation of those gusts and storms of rumour, detraction and envy; and a resolution not to be over sensible of all calumnies, unkindness, or injustice, but to believe that, by being preferred before other men, they have an obligation upon them to suffer more than other men would do, and that the best way to convince scandals and misreports is, by neglecting them, to appear not to have deserved them. And there is not a more troublesome inconvenient passion, or that which often draws more inconveniences with it, than that which proceeds from the indignation of being unjustly calumniated, and from the pride of an upright conscience, when men cannot endure to be spoken ill of when they have not deserved it: in which distemper, though they free themselves from the errors or infirmities with which they were traduced, they commonly discover others of which they had never been suspected. (VII, 283)

This is *moral* wisdom; and it underlies—is one with—the political wisdom. It is this, I think, that constitutes Clarendon's greatness as an historian: that there is a constant reference beyond politics—beyond, that is, the conflict of forces—to the human ground.

We touch here on Clarendon's representative significance. The wisdom expressed in the passages I have quoted grows not simply out of 'politics' but out of 'culture'; it is not merely a result of reading—though Clarendon had read widely in the classics; it is the product of a civilized tradition and of habits of civilized intercourse. We may return to the observations of character and motive. What is shown by Clarendon's firm grasp of the personal factor in history and his shrewd and subtle appraisal of character, is that he was the product of a society within which there was a highly developed sense of the person, a society for which personal and moral issues mattered, and which possessed a language in which these issues could be intelligently discussed.[1]

That, I think, is an observation that may be made with some assurance. There remains a need for a full scholarly study of Clarendon's milieu—of the milieu sketched in the opening chapters of his *Life*. There was the early acquaintance with Ben Jonson, Selden, Cotton, Thomas Carew and others— a London circle of scholars, poets, and wits. There was the later more intimate friendship with Falkland and the group that gathered at Great Tew—that 'college situated in a purer air': Sheldon, Morley, Earle, Hales, and Chillingworth, amongst others. Such a study would certainly establish the very great variety of interests and aptitudes represented in the circles that Clarendon frequented—poetry, history, law, philosophy, theology, and public affairs.[2] The Falkland group has of course a very special significance: it was not only a centre of humane learning, it was *the* centre of what—if we define our terms—we may call 'religious liberalism'.[3] The liberalism of these men was not so much a matter of 'advanced' theological views (they were

[1] Clarendon's style in the character studies is invariably firm as well as subtle, displaying none of that awkwardness that occasionally marks the more purely narrative portions of his history. Clarendon's appraisal of public figures normally includes some reference not only to their learning, or lack of it, but to their skill in 'discourse'.

[2] 'Mr Earles would frequently profess that he had got more useful learning by his conversation at Tew (the Lord Falkland's house) than he had at Oxford.' *The Life of Edward Earl of Clarendon, written by Himself*, edition of 1759, Vol. I, p. 51. *Characters of the Seventeenth Century*, ed. Nichol Smith, p. 169.

[3] 'There are few more curious problems in English history than that which these facts suggest. Why was it that religious liberalism in the seventeenth century was allied with political Toryism, whilst the most bigoted and narrow views of religion were held by the founders of our political liberties? We cannot at present enter upon this inquiry; but, in order to understand Clarendon, it is necessary to be aware of its existence, and to know that, though the highest of high Tories, he was anything but a bigot.'—Sir James Stephen, *Horae Sabbaticae*, First Series, p. 319.

devout and convinced members of the Church of England) as of
a temper of mind and an attitude towards the important theological and ecclesiastical questions then in debate. Clarendon
tells us of Falkland that 'he was so great an enemy to that passion
and uncharitableness which he saw produced by differences of
opinions in matters of religion, that in all those disputations with
priests and others of the Roman Church, he affected to manifest
all possible civility to their persons and estimation of their parts'
(VII, 221). 'In all those controversies, he had so dispassioned a
consideration, such a candour in his nature, and so profound a
charity in his conscience, that in those points in which he was in
his own judgment most clear, he never thought the worse, or in
any degree declined the familiarity of those who were of another
mind, which without question is an excellent temper for the
propagation and advancement of Christianity.'[1] Of Hales we
read: 'Nothing troubled him more than the brawls which were
grown from religion, and he therefore exceedingly detested the
tyranny of the Church of Rome, more for their imposing un-
charitably upon the consciences of other men, than for their
errors in their own opinions, and would often say, that he would
renounce the religion of the Church of England tomorrow if it
obliged him to believe that any other Christians should be
damned: and that nobody would conclude another man to be
damned, who did not wish him so: ... and he thought that pride
and passion more than conscience were the cause of all separation from each other's communion.'[2] Moderation of this kind,
based on conviction, is as far removed from indifference as it is
from fanaticism. It is a similar moderation and humanity that
displays itself in what we know of the political attitudes of
Falkland and his friends. None of them was a violent partisan.
'When there was any overture of peace, he [Falkland] would be
more erect, and vigorous, and exceedingly solicitous to press any

---

[1] *Life*, Vol. I, p. 43. *Characters of the Seventeenth Century*, p. 93.
[2] *Life*, Vol. I, p. 53. *Characters of the Seventeenth Century*, p. 172.

thing which he thought might promote it' [VII, 233]. It was Chillingworth who, preaching before the court at Oxford, described the contending parties as 'Publicans and Sinners on the one side against Scribes and Pharisees on the other'.[1] It is to the significance of this circle that the *History of the Rebellion*—regarded not simply as a history but as a document of the moral sensibility of the age—may direct our attention.

The *History of the Rebellion*, then, is an important document in the history of English civilization in the seventeenth century. But it is more than a document: it has an actual value. What its value for the present is, I think we may see if we put beside it a very different but in some ways comparable book, *The History of the Russian Revolution* by Leon Trotsky. Trotsky, like Clarendon, describes the genesis and course of great events in which he was one of the leading actors; and although his bias—like Clarendon's—is not in doubt, he too intended his book as a contribution to serious history. The differences in method and approach are revealing. Trotsky, like Marx, from whom his historical method is derived, is clearly the product of an age dominated by the idea of scientific law. His vigorous intellect works in terms of masses and social forces, and the slightest fluctuation in the main course of events is caught and pinned into place as a logically necessary exception.[2] If we feel that Claren-

---

[1] J. A. R. Marriott, *The Life and Times of Lucius Cary, Viscount Falkland*, p. 248. Marriott also quotes Fuller, preaching in London: 'Think not that the King's army is like Sodom, not ten righteous men in it, and the other army like Zion, consisting all of saints'.

[2] Characteristic phrases are, 'the law of combined development', 'shifts in the correlation of class forces', 'the molecular process in the masses', 'the inevitable dynamic of a revolutionary process', 'the resultant of the composition of forces'. 'What distinguished Bolshevism was that it subordinated the subjective (*sic*) goal, the defence of the interests of the popular masses, to the laws of revolution as an objectively conditioned process. The scientific discovery of these laws, and first of all those which govern the movement of popular masses, constituted the basis of the Bolshevik strategy.'—*The History of the Russian Revolution*, translated by Max Eastman, Vol. II, p. 309.

don sometimes mistakenly attributes representative acts to purely personal motives, in reading Trotsky we are constantly aware of the absence of the personal—especially of the irrational, or non-rational—motives that certainly played a part in the actions he describes.[1] Nor is there a single person—not even Lenin—who appears in the book as anything more than a bloodless embodiment of political will or of some social category. The result is that although the *History of the Russian Revolution* is packed with detail the total effect is of something abstract and schematized. One cannot resist the conclusion that the pattern, so vigorously asserted in its complex detail, is to a large extent imposed.

The question here is not which of our two historians was more 'correct' in his analysis of political problems. In Clarendon's day, as in Trotsky's, men contested with passion for their own ideas of the best forms of government. They will continue to contest, and there is no means of securing uniformity of opinion. The question on which we might hope to secure some measure of agreement from men of different parties concerns the *relation* of political thinking to the general life of the community. Of any analyst of politics, as of any political leader, we may ask, What are the implications of his habitual modes of thought in terms of that wider human life, which only from one angle appears as political life? For Trotsky, analysis of past events is plainly a tool to be used in shaping the future. 'Revolutions', he says, 'take place according to certain laws. This does not mean that the masses in action are aware of the laws of revolution, but it does mean that the changes in mass consciousness are not accidental, but are subject to an objective necessity which is capable of theoretic explanation, *and thus makes both prophecy and leadership possible*' (Vol. II, p. 10). Now if the analysis is partial, in the sense

[1] As an analyst of crowd behaviour he could have learnt something from the account of the Milan bread riots in Manzoni's *The Betrothed*.

that only data of a certain kind pass through the sieve, the 'prophecy' and the 'leadership' are equally suspect. Occasionally Trotsky lets the cat out of the bag. 'The proletariat was the chief motive force of revolution,' he says. 'At the same time the revolution was giving shape to the proletariat. And the proletariat was badly in need of this' (Vol. I, p. 426). Substitute for the abstraction, 'the revolution', the more specific term, 'the party agitators' (as is plain from the immediately following pages we are entitled to do) and the scientific bluff is called. Similar sleights are not infrequent. 'It would seem as though the soviets, elected by a part of the city's population, should have less power and influence than the dumas, elected by the whole population. But the dialectic of the revolutionary process has demonstrated that in certain historic conditions the part is incomparably greater than the whole' (Vol. II, p. 303). And in the concluding chapters of the *History* there are some revealing passages on the difference between 'formal democracy' (*sc.* democracy) and 'authentic democracy' (*sc.* the Party dictatorship). Such passages, which Clarendon would have considered an abuse of reason, reveal fully the wider implications of which I have spoken. The blindness to everything in life but some schematized abstractions is the disease of a mind that thinks solely in terms of power and that therefore, of necessity, propagates the idea of power as the sole concern of political man. Trotsky is the embodiment of political will masquerading as destiny or impersonal law.[1]

---

[1] 'In practice,' Trotsky writes, 'a reformist party considers unshakable the foundations of that which it intends to reform. It thus inevitably submits to the ideas and morals of the ruling class. . . . Bolshevism created the type of the authentic revolutionary who subordinates to historic goals irreconcilable with contemporary society the conditions of his personal existence, his ideas, and his moral judgments (Vol. III, p. 166). That sounds very fine. Unfortunately the 'historic goals' that sound so solid are in fact nothing more than goals existing in the minds of those who proclaim them. When they are invoked to absolve men from the need for personal moral judgment,

Civilization and its products are in some ways analogous to the organic processes of nature. The humus of civilization—the worked top soil—is composed of attitudes, interests, moral judgments, habits of perception and response. Like the actual humus, this soil needs to be kept 'in good heart' if new growth is to occur; it can be impoverished, and it can be destroyed. Those who elect to discuss man's collective life have therefore a responsibility over and above their responsibility as recorders of events or promulgators of a point of view. When an influential political writer, by his underlying assumptions no less than by his overt judgments, commits himself to a view in which 'everything includes itself in power, power into will', he is destroying the very basis of any future good to which he may pay lip-service; he impoverishes the soil and debilitates the future. When he is not only an influential writer but a political leader and a representative political type, one may in all seriousness begin to think in terms of cultural erosion.

Considerations such as these may help to focus the present relevance of an historian who is sometimes dubbed, in the slack modern phrase, a reactionary. In the way in which Clarendon wrote about politics he helped to keep alive attitudes and habits of mind that are, in the long run, more important than any programme. We value him less for his political conclusions than for the manner of his approach to those conclusions. He believed in certain intellectual and moral principles, 'and integrity above

---

there is little need to speculate concerning the impulses that rush in to fill the void thus created.

> Tempting region *that*
> For Zeal to enter and refresh herself,
> Where passions had the privilege to work,
> And never hear the sound of their own names.
>
> Wordsworth, *The Prelude*, XI, ll. 228–31.

I should like to refer the reader to Mr G. H. Bantock's essay, 'Planning and Popularization', in *Scrutiny*, Vol. XIV, No. 3; also included in Mr Bantock's *Freedom and Authority in Education.*

all'.[1] He had a genuine humility in the face of events, not expecting 'a greater certitude in the consultation of business than the business of this world is capable of'. Above all, he had a keen and profound sense of the person, even of his opponents as persons, not simply as representatives of a category. For these reasons, as I have tried to show, he is a source of political wisdom of a kind not easily come by. That we may often disagree with his judgments does not matter. What matters is that we should be aware of the qualities—inherent in the handling of his material —that were to contribute to the more lasting achievements of civilization long after the political cause that he supported was lost. To be responsive to such qualities, and ourselves to foster such qualities in our political thinking, offers the only alternative to a progressive deterioration of public life to which those who are concerned for personal values cannot afford to be indifferent.

[1] 'And though it hath been, and will be, always necessary to admit to those Councils some men of great power that will not take the pains to have great parts, yet the number of the whole should not be too great, and the capacities and qualities of the most should be fit for business; that is, either for judgment or despatch, or for one of them at least; and integrity above all' (III, 53).

Historical Scholarship and the
Interpretation of Shakespeare

i

IN *English Poetry: a Critical Introduction*, F. W. Bateson
wrote:

> The readers . . . that the poet is implicitly addressing *determine* to
> a considerable degree the kind of poem that he is writing. It
> follows that to understand a poem's meaning today we need to be
> able to identify ourselves as far as possible with its original
> readers, the poet's contemporaries, whose ideal response to the
> poem in fact constitutes its meaning.

A good deal of Shakespeare scholarship and Elizabethan scholarship generally has in recent years worked in the spirit of this
remark. The results are impressive, and the critic or interpreter
of Shakespeare cannot ignore them. Shakespeare wanted neither
education nor art, and even the unscholarly reader will read with
more profit if he knows something of the ideas with which
Shakespeare was in contact, and even, perhaps, of the terms of
art in which Elizabethan poetry and drama were conceived. Yet
as one watches the successive waves of Shakespearean and
Elizabethan scholarship, each changing place with that which
went before, one feels uneasy. It is not that the attempt to interpret Shakespeare in contemporary (*sc.* Elizabethan) terms is
intrinsically unprofitable—far from it: it is simply that the claims
that are sometimes made for 'scholarship' as against 'criticism'
are excessive, that there is a danger of substituting accumulated
'knowledge about' for a living responsiveness; and that the
search for 'ideal' contemporary meanings and implications *tends*
to obscure the essential nature of art, and so to make particular
works of art, such as Shakespeare's plays, less potently available

and fructifying than they ought to be. I may state here my own conviction, as against Mr Bateson, that the meanings of a poem are not exhausted by the meanings it may have had for its original readers (who, as Lascelles Abercrombie remarked, did not respond as one man), adding too that the meanings it had for the original audience cannot in any case be identified with the meanings of which they were fully conscious. I shall return to these points; but first I should like to suggest by example how the historical approach, pursued as a means of interpretation, tends, by the very nature of its undertaking, to obscure as well as to elucidate Shakespeare's plays.

Shakespeare's Use of Learning: an Inquiry into the Growth of his Mind and Art, by Virgil K. Whitaker, is a valuable contribution to Shakespeare scholarship. I am not here concerned with Dr Whitaker's estimate of the extent of Shakespeare's learning: he comes down judiciously in favour of a Shakespeare whose interests slowly broadened from popular learning to philosophic ideas, who possessed considerable knowledge of contemporary psychology and theology, but who never read widely. Nor would I wish to challenge Dr Whitaker's insistence of the formative influence on the greater plays of a body of traditional ideas, transmitted largely, it is suggested, by the first book of Hooker's *Of the Laws of Ecclesiastical Polity*; it is certainly a reasonable contention that 'Macbeth is a greater play than *Richard III* not so much because Shakespeare knew more about the theatre as because he had developed a new understanding of life in terms of traditional Christian thought' (p. vii). What I am concerned with is the terms in which Dr Whitaker develops this thesis, for they seem to me characteristic of the 'historical' school.

The following are representative quotations:

Finally, about the turn of the century, his interests shifted markedly to the philosophical and theological interpretation of life which Christianity had erected during the Middle Ages upon

139

the basis of Plato, Aristotle, and the Stoics, the Scriptures, and St Augustine. Most of the tragedies are constructed to study the working out of these principles in human conduct. . . . (p. 11)

[In the earlier plays] the plot determined the characters. Beginning with *Hamlet* the exact opposite is true. In using *Plutarch*, who furnished biographies that are really character studies worked out in terms of an elaborate ethical theory, Shakespeare made relatively few changes. . . . But he reshaped his other sources drastically in order to make the action reveal characters that illustrate or conform to philosophic concepts, the best examples of this process being *Macbeth* and *Lear*. (p. 179)

The earlier plays merely adapt a source narrative to stage presentation. The problem comedies try to superimpose philosophic interpretation upon material developed by the same easygoing methods, and trouble results. The tragedies, on the other hand, reshape the plot to fit a predetermined character problem. (p. 179)

'The tragedies are constructed to study the working out of these principles . . .', 'characters that illustrate or conform to philosophic concepts', 'the tragedies reshape the plot to fit a predetermined character problem'—do not these phrases make the plays seem to be more schematic, more deliberately intellectual, less exploratory, imaginative, and creative, than they actually are? The imagination can use intellectual formulations, and Shakespeare's poetic thought was certainly nourished and clarified by the best of what he read (including perhaps Hooker)[1];

[1] Leone Vivante (*English Poetry*, pp. 122–3) has some suggestive remarks on the distinction between what T. S. Eliot in his Preface to the same volume calls 'poetic thinking' and 'the thought of the poet'. Signor Vivante's suggestion that we should 'consider (adopting Coleridge's words) "truth operative", truth "original—more accurately . . . ever-originating", as compared with a process of thought in which the author is sharply distinct from his subject-matter' is decidedly relevant to the present discussion. (As a matter of fact, Coleridge's 'truth operative' is part of a quotation from Davenant—'truth operative, and by effects continually alive'. See *Biographia Literaria*, ed. Shawcross, Vol. II, pp. 101–2).

but to see his imaginative exploration as though it were merely the application of already formed concepts is to miss the dimension of depth, the personal vibrancy, that prevents, or should prevent, us from speaking of *Lear* or *Macbeth* in terms of the application of 'a formula for tragedy of moral choice' (p. 248). T. S. Eliot, in his essay on John Ford, long ago gave us the necessary corrective when he wrote:

> It is suggested, then, that a dramatic poet cannot create characters of the greatest intensity of life unless his personages, in their reciprocal actions and behaviour in their story, are somehow dramatizing, but in no obvious form, an action or struggle for harmony in the soul of the poet.[1]

It is that central dynamic that Dr Whitaker's method, his very terminology, implicitly ignores.

And corresponding to the rather rigid externalizing assumptions about the nature of the poetic process is a complementary distortion of the nature of the work of art in relation to the reader, of what the act of appreciation means. Dr Whitaker writes interestingly about *Troilus and Cressida*, 'the keystone in the arch of Shakespeare's intellectual development' (p. 195)—and indeed it is always refreshing to have this play treated as an intellectual structure rather than as an uncontrolled outburst of cynicism. Certainly it is a play of 'ideas'. But how are the ideas treated? How does the play demand that we should take them? Dr Whitaker holds that in the consultation of the Greek generals (I, iii), containing Ulysses' speech on degree, and in the parallel council of the Trojan leaders (II, ii), containing Hector's exposition of 'the moral laws of nature and of nation', 'Shakespeare was more interested in the ideas themselves than in the movement of his plot' (p. 196), and he proceeds to expound the implications and background (Elyot, the Homilies, and Hooker)

---

[1] *Selected Essays* (London, 1932), p. 196. It is in the same essay that Mr Eliot puts forward the idea of the whole of Shakespeare's work as '*one* poem . . . united by one significant, consistent, and developing personality'.

of these ideas. The exposition is relevant and sound, but the play is, after all, something more than the dramatic presentation of philosophic ideas, and it is the play as a whole—the play as an imaginative structure, permeated and not simply as it were buttressed by thought—that determines how we shall take the ideas that it contains. And the play as a whole certainly does not endorse Ulysses, for all his classic exposition of the traditional conception of an ordered universe. Neither does it endorse Troilus, whose subjectivism is the complementary opposite of the rationalism of the Greeks. Two attitudes to life are put in dramatic contrast; but the point is that they *are* attitudes to life, each of them containing emotional as well as intellectual elements—for even Troilus can rationalize his feelings, and even Ulysses' speech on degree needs to be seen in the context of what he does, says, and implies elsewhere. The play, in short, makes complex demands and asks of us something more than the ability to pick out ideas, however significant in themselves.[1] I should say that it is only in the light of a full imaginative responsiveness to the play as a dramatic poem, in which Elizabethan ideas are assimilated and used, but never merely applied, that we can see the full significance of Hector's admirable defence of the law of nature, to which Dr Whitaker rightly gives so much attention.

Of the failure of imagination that seems almost inevitable when the critic works too persistently and exclusively in terms of clearly formulated ideas two further examples may be given.

2 *Henry IV*, despite its parallels of structure, contains statements of contemporary learning of a kind which is completely absent from Part 1, so that it seems to have been written from Shakespeare's intellect, whereas Part 1 came from his heart. . . . An important part of this learning is the concept of order and of natural law. For the first time the vague hints of the earlier plays give way to explicit statement. (p. 169)

[1] See my essay on the play in *Some Shakespearean Themes*.

142

Now *2 Henry IV*, is, I agree, different from the first Part, and I am sure that Shakespeare's intellect was active in the making of it. But so was his heart. And if we find Part 2 more 'philosophic' than Part 1, this is due not merely to any 'explicit statement' of ideas of order but to Shakespeare's imaginative vision (expressed in the whole play, which includes Shallow and Wart and even old Double, as well as the politicals) of life subject to time and change. And surely the condition of our recognizing *Macbeth* as 'Shakespeare's greatest monument to the ethical system that his age inherited from Western Christianity and the classical world' (p. 299) is not that we should exclude from our consciousness all that does not *explicitly* demonstrate the identity of the unnatural, the irrational, and the immoral—all, that is, that cannot be formulated and expounded in strictly rational terms. Yet this is oddly implied by the qualification that Dr Whitaker thinks it necessary to make to his praise of that tragedy.

> There is . . . something a little too pat about the relationship between man's sins and the universal disorder as Shakespeare presents it. Macbeth violates the law of nature by murdering a man who is his king, his kinsman, and his guest. At once all nature behaves unnaturally. What the play gives us is at times closer to the pathetic fallacy than to a genuinely philosophic view of the interrelationship between man and the rest of creation. (p. 209)

The unnatural behaviour of nature in *Macbeth*—

> The night has been unruly; where we lay,
> Our chimneys were blown down. . . .
>
> Is't night's predominance, or the day's shame,
> That darkness does the face of earth entomb,
> When living light should kiss it?

—is obviously one of the ways in which the inner darkness and disorder of sin is evoked and defined. Thus the two passages just quoted are nearer to St John's 'He that loveth his brother abideth in the light. . . . But he that hateth his brother is in darkness and walketh in darkness', or to Milton's

> not only tears
> Rain'd at their eyes, but high winds worse within
> Began to rise, high passions, anger, hate,
> Mistrust, suspicion . . .

than they are to any form of the pathetic fallacy.

I have spent some time on this book, deliberately and unfairly ignoring much that is valuable in it, because it seems to me representative of a whole approach to Shakespeare, and because it offers an example of what is likely to happen if you set out to interpret a great writer of the past exclusively in the intellectual terms of his own day; if, instead of starting with Shakespeare's plays, your own direct experience of Shakespeare's plays, and working back to what most deeply nourished them in the thought, the mental habits and the tradition of the time, you invoke a conceptual framework which you proceed to show the plays as illustrating. The attraction of the historical or reconstructive procedure is of course that it seems to approach something like a guaranteed meaning—*the* meaning in the minds of an ideal audience contemporary with the plays—and thereby to offer an escape from the uncertainty of merely personal interpretation and criticism, which varies not only with the taste of the age but with the predilections of the individual: now that Elizabethan scholarship has come of age and stands so sturdily on its own feet, our major effort must be directed to re-creating an 'Elizabethan' Shakespeare. But there are, I think, other reasons besides those so far touched on why, in the face of such advice, we should maintain a certain reserve.

ii

If we believe that the attempt to reconstruct the Elizabethan
or Renaissance meanings of Shakespeare's plays is almost inevitably attended by the danger of obscuring their imaginative
life, does this mean that we must simply accept the fact of
different meanings for different generations, or indeed for different individuals living at the same time? I think it does—but with
a qualification that is as important as it is obvious. No one who
has made his own the idea of a critical discipline embodied in
Matthew Arnold's formula, 'To see the object as in itself it
really is', is likely to accept the spineless relativism of 'So many
men, so many minds'. For the worth of any interpretation or
judgment of literary value depends on the mind that makes it,
its lucidity, discipline, and capacity for genuinely confronting
its object.

In his classic lecture, 'A Plea for the Liberty of Interpreting',[1]
Lascelles Abercrombie insisted, as it is insisted here, that a work
of art can only be judged in the light of what we ourselves find
there. 'To limit interpretation to what the play may have meant
to Elizabethans is, frankly, to exclude the existence of the play
as a work of art; for as a work of art it does not exist in what it
may have meant to someone else, but in what it means to me:
that is the only way it can exist.' Abercrombie is, however,
quite clear about the reasonable limits of interpretation:

> By liberty of interpretation I do not mean liberty to read into a
> play of Shakespeare's whatever feeling or idea a modern reader
> may loosely and accidentally associate with its subject: associate it,
> that is, not because he found it in the play, but because some idio-
> syncracy of his own suggested it and irresponsibly brought it
> in from his private world. But I do mean that anything which may
> be found in that art, even if it is only the modern reader who can

[1] Annual Shakespeare Lecture of the British Academy, 1930 (*Proceedings
of the British Academy*, XVI); reprinted in *Aspects of Shakespeare*.

find it there, may legitimately be taken as its meaning. *Judge by results*, I say; not by the results of reverie, which the poem merely sets going, and in which attention may ramble anywhere it pleases, for that is not criticism at all; but certainly by any result that may come of living in the art of the play and attending to everything it consists of: and I say that, so long as it keeps within that boundary, there is no proper ground for objection if this attention seems to be modern in its nature.

And again,

> When I say that a play exists in what it means to any one who will receive it, the implication is plain, that everything is excluded from that existence which is not given by the author's technique. The existence of a work of art is completed by the recipient's *attention* to what the author says to him; whatever may come in through *inattention* to that does not belong to the art at all.

What this admirable statement means is that when, in Shakespeare criticism, we have discounted everything that clearly results from indiscipline, from inattention, prejudice or whimsy, we are still confronted with interpretations of the same material that differ widely one from another. But instead of being disturbed by this, we should rather rejoice at the evidence it affords of the perennial quickening activity of all genuine art.

To examine all the criticism of one of Shakespeare's greater plays—all, that is, that bears the impress of a mind genuinely at work; to trace how some of the major changes in what intelligent people have found there have come about; to show how shifts of interest or emphasis have brought into view fresh sets of relationships within the play, relationships and significances that were 'there' all the time, yet not visible until a particular viewpoint had altered, as though the play were a many-faceted crystal refracting the light differently according to the way it is held; to see how even individual words and phrases can suddenly reveal a richness previously latent and unguessed at:—this would be one way of suggesting what is meant when we speak of the perpetually generative power of a great work of art. But even without such demonstration the fact is clear enough. 'The existence of a work of art'—to quote Lascelles Abercrombie once more—'is not material at all, but spiritual. It is a continually creative existence, for it exists by continually creating experience.'

That this power is operative even when the cast of mind, the prevailing assumptions, are quite alien to those of the Elizabethan period, is evident from the genuine praise of Shakespeare throughout the eighteenth century. It is of course true that prejudices regarding language and decorum (themselves deriving from wider prejudices and presuppositions) did then prevent anything like a full exposure to some vitally important (we may say central) aspects of Shakespeare's genius—as we see from the list of 'considerable imperfections' with which Joseph Warton concluded his *Adventurer* papers in praise of *King Lear*[1]:

> The plot of Edmund against his brother, which distracts the attention, and destroys the unity of the fable; the cruel and horrid extinction of Gloucester's eyes, which ought not to be exhibited on the stage; the utter improbability of Gloucester's imagining, though blind, that he had leapt down from Dover cliff; and some passages that are too turgid and full of strained metaphors; are faults which the warmest admirers of Shakespeare will find it difficult to excuse. I know not, also, whether the cruelty of the daughters is not painted with circumstances too savage and unnatural; for it is not sufficient to say, that this monstrous barbarity is founded on historical truth, if we recollect the just observation of Boileau,
>
> Le vray peut quelquefois n'être pas vraisemblable.
> Some truth may be too strong to be believed.

This well suggests the nature of the presuppositions, both general and specific, that obscured Shakespeare's tragic vision in the

---

[1] *The Adventurer* (1752-4), Nos. 113, 116, 122.

eighteenth century. The point is, however, that they could not completely obscure it. Dr Johnson approved—at least, he refused to condemn—Tate's ending for *King Lear*; but it is impossible to doubt that his mind derived substantial nourishment from 'this deservedly celebrated' drama: 'So powerful is the current of the poet's imagination, that the mind, which once ventures within it, is hurried irresistibly along.' Clearly the play *meant* a great deal to Johnson, even though what it meant—the precise ways in which his mind 'ventured within it'—was something very different from what it means to, say, Mr Robert Heilman.[1]

It may of course be claimed that what has since informed our consciousness—romantic inwardness (Lamb's 'While we read ..., we see not Lear, but we are Lear'), the accumulated insights of different critics regarding the powers of language, a vastly increased knowledge of Elizabethan dramatic conventions and intellectual background (the fruits of that very scholarship towards which I have hinted some reserve)—that all this has made more of the Shakespeare experience available, has indeed brought us closer to the Elizabethan Shakespeare. It may be so; but so far as the present argument is concerned there are other relevant considerations. One, already glanced at, is that even for the unhistorical eighteenth century Shakespeare was a genuine possession: indeed what the men of that century lost from their ignorance of the Elizabethan setting was at least partially compensated by the very fact that their approach was *not* that of the 'Elizabethan specialist' but that of the moralist, man of the world, or common reader. Another, more important, is that when we call to mind representative samples of twentieth-century criticism, by writers most of whom are in possession of the advantages of modern scholarship, we are still forced to the same conclusion regarding the nature of 'the object'. I don't for one moment mean that all writers on, say, *King Lear* are equally 'right': criticism recognizes degrees of sensitiveness and

[1] See *This Great Stage: Image and Structure in 'King Lear'*.

centrality. But we certainly cannot assume that if all our critics were equally sensitive, intelligent and informed they would present us with the same interpretation of the play. Clearly they would not. And even if by chance they did—if all their findings harmoniously agreed instead of sometimes tugging different ways—the '*Lear* experience' of each of them, and of each of their readers, would still be a unique, individual experience. The assimilation of a play into a particular individual context— a context of life experience, which includes the experience of other books—is a necessary part of its meaning, even though that meaning is so far from being a merely private possession that criticism is not only a possible but a profitable activity. We come out of course at a paradox, beautifully suggested in Wallace Stevens' address to the 'Supreme Fiction'—encountered, it will be remembered,

> In the uncertain light of single, certain truth,
> Equal in living changingness to the light
> In which I meet you. . . .

It is with these lines in mind that Marius Bewley comments[1]:

From Stevens' work as a whole we know that one of the intrinsic elements of the imagination (as of life) is motion and change. . . . 'Single, certain truth' is in constant motion, is glimpsed and realized in moments of vital, vivid apprehension, and this act of apprehension itself may constitute ontologically a part, and perhaps a large part, of the truth.

Transposing this gloss into terms immediately relevant to the present discussion, we may say of Shakespeare, as of literature generally, that what is 'there' for intelligent discussion— something belonging to the more-than-individual world of shared experience—exists only in individual apprehensions which themselves, in some sense, contribute to its being.

[1] *The Complex Fate*, p. 182.

Now it seems to me that it is only on condition of our not forgetting this truth that we can hope to get into perspective the large amount of work that is being done in reconstructing the Elizabethan background, and to understand something of the relation of Shakespeare's plays to contemporary and traditional ideas. Shakespeare, we may now safely assume, was not unlearned; he had a naturally philosophic mind; he was in touch with the ideas of his age. But those ideas entered into his plays in so far as they met an intense inner need to find meanings in experience. They were tested and assimilated as part of the 'action or struggle for harmony in the soul of the poet' of which T. S. Eliot speaks. And encountered and assimilated in this way they ceased to be concepts to be applied or illustrated: they became elements of imaginative power, 'united by one significant, consistent, and developing personality'.

Now in this personal exploratory process there is no doubt that Shakespeare found his way to certain traditional ideas of great importance. Various critics have shown the significance of traditional ideas concerning the law of nature in *King Lear*, and W. C. Curry, in *Shakespeare's Philosophical Patterns*, has shown how *Macbeth* is saturated with moral and metaphysical conceptions deriving from the Schoolmen. But the point is that these ideas are never merely accepted and applied; they are re-lived; their adequacy is tested in a full and personal exposure to life, and only then are they assimilated into a work of art with a life of its own. Thus *Macbeth*, as Professor Curry insists, certainly contains the idea of the negative quality of evil which was developed within the framework of Scholastic philosophy. But the idea is not stated as an idea to be illustrated. It is embodied in the unique combination of perceptions, insights, and feelings that is *Macbeth*; it is apprehended simultaneously in sensory, emotional, and intellectual terms; it is made vivid by the contrasting presence of images of life; and in the intense pressure of the imaginative process the idea acquires a new dynamic. In other words, however much Shakespeare may have profited from conceptions sharpened and made viable by theologians and philosophers (by whatever ways these reached him), there is no question of the dramatic embodiment or illustration of ideas that remain as it were external to the poet. The creative insights of *Lear* and *Macbeth* and the later plays were won in a direct encounter with life's problems, and there is the felt pressure of life in the forms in which they are embodied. That is why they can 'continually create experience'.

iv

It is time to draw together the threads of this paper and to attempt a direct answer to the question I began by raising concerning the value of historical scholarship in the study of literature. Can we now see how the scholarly exploration of the sixteenth-century climate of opinion may meet fruitfully the criticism of Shakespeare's plays as living works of the imagination, as something other than repositories of Elizabethan doctrine? I think we can. Starting from our own direct experience of the plays (and without that we have nothing to start from) we are interested, first, in anything that may make that experience deeper and more vivid, and then, but only then, in anything that may illuminate the relation between living art and the civilization behind it, and so give us a firmer grasp of the nature of a living tradition. With that starting point, and with these interests, we have some means of distinguishing the value of different kinds of 'background' study.

The common reader, bent on understanding Shakespeare's plays to the best of his ability, will not of course take a superior

attitude to any kind of honest scholarship. There are many pre-
liminaries to criticism that only scholarship can provide: information about stage conditions, dramatic conventions, the basic
contemporary meanings of some words, and so on. And if
you are genuinely interested in Shakespeare almost any reliable
information about his age is likely to come in handy—so long,
that is, as you do not allow yourself to become cluttered up with
miscellaneous information as a substitute for the more exacting
task of reading poetry: remembering also that a little personal
reading of Shakespeare's greater contemporaries is more profitable than too much reading of 'background' books.

In the second place, even as common readers, we need to know
something about the reading and listening habits of the poet's
first audience. I have in mind such things as L. A. Cormican's
suggestive account of the habits of mind fostered by a familiarity
with the Liturgy.[1] We need to know these things, not so that
we can attempt to make ourselves into Elizabethans (we cannot
do that), but so that we can cultivate comparable skills, a comparable flexibility of mind, in our own approach to Shakespeare's
meanings.

Finally—and here we come to the crux of the matter—aware
of the 'philosophical' aspect of Shakespeare's work, we shall find
that we want to know something of the traditional moral philosophy which nourished, without confining, his imagination—
whilst yet avoiding the danger of substituting such knowledge
for the direct experience of the plays, or of supposing that these
can be reduced to anything like an illustration or demonstration
of past systems of thought.[2] What we want to know about, I

[1] L. A. Cormican, 'Medieval Idiom in Shakespeare': (1) 'Shakespeare and
the Liturgy', (2) 'Shakespeare and the Medieval Ethic'. *Scrutiny*, XVII, 3
and 4. See also S. L. Bethell, *Shakespeare and the Popular Dramatic Tradition.*
[2] 'To apply medieval ideas to our understanding of Shakespearean
tragedy is no mere matter of supplying footnotes to particular lines or
references; it is a matter of grasping a whole mentality which is implicit, and
often explicit, in the plays.'—L. A. Cormican, loc. cit.

suppose, are those major elements in the thought of the time that themselves have a perpetually generative power—that is, that are capable of nourishing the greatest diversity of minds, of illuminating ever fresh combinations of circumstances. And the condition of our fruitfully applying these ideas to our study of Shakespeare is that we should *not* approach them as Shakespearean scholars bent on reconstructing a merely historical background, but—paradoxically—that we should study them for themselves, responding to them as themselves actual and vivifying. Thus when Professor Curry describes for us the traditional background of the metaphysics of evil in *Macbeth*, we value his work because it puts us in touch with creative insights, developed by religious teachers and philosophers, that apply in any age, and so enables us to grasp more firmly what is essential to *Macbeth* as an ever-present work of imagination. When Miss Pope shows us how, in *Measure for Measure*, Shakespeare cuts through common confusions of his time regarding the relations of justice and mercy, going straight back to the inspiration of the Gospels,[1] we are faced with something quite different from a literary 'source', something that cannot possibly be relegated to 'history' but that directly impinges on the here and now: and the very condition of our seeing the play in relation to the Sermon on the Mount is that both play and Sermon should be imaginatively apprehended as present facts of experience. When, helped for example by Professor A. P. d'Entrèves' admirable little book on Natural Law, we try to bring traditional thinking on this subject into relation with our experience of *King Lear*— with what J. F. Danby calls 'Shakespeare's Doctrine of Nature' —it is the present, and not merely the historical, significance of the conceptions of Natural Law thinking that we need to have in mind. When we try to find the roots of what I should call

[1] Elizabeth Pope, 'The Renaissance Background of *Measure for Measure*', *Shakespeare Survey*, II, 66 ff. See also G. Wilson Knight, '*Measure for Measure* and the Gospels', in *The Wheel of Fire*.

Shakespeare's personalist approach to politics, it is with a sense of the present relevance of the medieval insistence on the moral foundations of politics. And so with all the life-bearing ideas of Shakespeare's age, whether we try to get in touch with them by the help of scholars or whether we confront them directly in the great books that nourished the Elizabethan mind and the work of original thinkers of the period such as Hooker. Like calls to like, and living art can best be studied in the light of living ideas. Such 'historical' study as we find necessary would not presuppose as its ultimate aim the restoration of Renaissance meanings. For the most part it would not be 'historical' at all in any limited sense: it would be predominantly the study of the varying forms—the varying apprehensions—of the great perennial truths. I suggest that if we guide our studies in the light of some such ideal as this we shall be better equipped to see Shakespeare's work for what it is: a unique creation, nourished by the complex of living thoughts that we call tradition, but with such depth of life that its essential meanings need to be elicited afresh in each generation—'so rammed with life', as Jonson said of Virgil's poetry,

—so rammed with life,
That it shall gather strength of life, with being.

Idea and Symbol: Some Hints from Coleridge

IN *The Statesman's Manual* Coleridge gives an account of
symbols and the symbolic process that is well known to all
students of his thought.

> The histories and political economy of the present and preceding
> century partake in the general contagion of its mechanic philo-
> sophy, and are the product of an unenlivened generalizing under-
> standing. In the Scriptures they are the living educts of the
> imagination; of that reconciling and mediatory power, which,
> incorporating the reason in images of the sense, and organizing
> (as it were) the flux of the senses by the permanence and self-
> circling energies of the reason, gives birth to a system of symbols,
> harmonious in themselves, and consubstantial with the truths of
> which they are the conductors. . . . An allegory is but a transla-
> tion of abstract notions into a picture-language, which is itself
> nothing but an abstraction from objects of the senses. . . . On the
> other hand a symbol . . . is characterized by the translucence of
> the special in the individual, or of the general in the especial, or
> of the universal in the general. Above all by the translucence of
> the eternal through and in the temporal. It always partakes of the
> reality which it renders intelligible; and while it enunciates the
> whole, abides itself as a living part in that unity, of which it is
> the representative.[1]

This account follows an eloquent passage on the seminal power
of ideas—ideas which, as Coleridge is at pains to insist, can be
'suggested and awakened' but, unlike the conceptions of the

[1] *Political Tracts of Wordsworth, Coleridge, Shelley*, edited, with an Introduction, by R. J. White, pp. 24-5.

understanding, cannot be adequately expressed by words[1]—and it is plain that for Coleridge the function of symbols is to handle meanings that cannot be conceptually grasped. 'An IDEA, in the *highest* sense of that word, cannot be conveyed but by a *symbol*.'[2]

Now it seems to me that there is very much that is useful in those passages, especially perhaps the association of symbols with what Coleridge calls the 'self-circling energies of the reason'. This however is something to which I shall return. The question that I wish to take up first is how one may be said to take meanings in any way that is not loosely subjective from symbols that, by definition, are not susceptible of the clarity and distinctness proper to the understanding. There is no need to make a mystery of this. Certainly there are some symbols, of the kind that Jung calls archetypal, that seems to draw their power from sources well beyond the power of direct conscious inspection; and if I think that the invocation of archetypes can sometimes make literary criticism too easy (curiously enough, more shallow instead of more profound), I am also prepared to agree that images of this kind are sometimes to be found in great literature, and that we need to recognize their 'archetypal' quality. But in clarifying our sense of how verbal symbols have meaning we can go a very long way indeed before we need invoke these entirely unanalysable psychic entities. In literature, at all events—and I think the same applies to religious writing —the meaning of anything that we recognize as a symbol is determined by a context. To be more exact, there are two overlapping contexts within which meaning takes place: there is the context from which the symbol emerges—namely the work within which it occurs, and the yet wider context of meanings which the artist draws on in making his work; and there is the

[1] See, for example, *On the Constitution of Church and State According to the Idea of Each*, ed. H. N. Coleridge (1839), p. 176.
[2] *Biographia Literaria*, ed. J. Shawcross, Vol. I, p. 100.

context into which it enters—namely the moving and developing life of the person responding. Neither of these is a simple notion, but if we examine them we may find a way of giving some account of the way symbols work, and of distinguishing various degrees of power.

The given context is, in the first place, what is made by the writer; indeed it is obvious that in discussions of this kind it is only for convenience that we can refer to 'a symbol' as a sort of extractable unit in any work of imaginative literature. The symbol in Blake's poem is not 'a tiger', it is

> Tyger! Tyger! burning bright
> In the forests of the night,

— and so on through all six stanzas. Blake's symbolic tiger is Blake's poem.[1] That is obvious enough, but we may as well remind ourseves that with symbols, as with every other aspect of a literary work, everything depends on the artist's genius; it is that alone, in its specific working, that can make his symbols nodal points of meaning. And even if we confine our attention to works of considerable stature there are distinctions to be made: good intentions are not enough; and we can properly distinguish between, on the one hand, the generative 'life' symbols of

---

[1] As Martin Foss says of metaphor in his *Symbol and Metaphor in Human Experience* (p. 61), 'Metaphor is a process of tension and energy, manifested in the process of language, not in the single word.' Particular works of art, moreover, may have a symbolic quality or aspect, whether or not, in any instance, we find it convenient to isolate the more obvious focal points of symbolic meaning. In a discussion of symbolism in the American novel, Marius Bewley writes: '. . . the excessive claims made for symbolism today have a tendency to blind us to those subtle, but more modest, achievements of symbolic technique where the method itself is working quietly hand in hand with the materials and pressures of external reality, and where the symbolic process is not defined by the operation of some one overwhelming symbol such as Moby Dick, but is a quality of imagery and organization in the texture of the prose, gradually gathering towards a concentration of effect that is, in fact, a symbol although it may not overtly present itself as one.'—*The Eccentric Design: Form in the Classic American Novel*, p. 106.

Macbeth, or the significance taken on by the White Whale in *Moby Dick,* and, on the other, the comparatively inert, worked out symbolism of *The Golden Bowl.*

But although the writer makes his own immediate context (and this indeed is of fundamental importance), beyond the work itself, entering into it and in part determining it, is a far wider context. T. S. Eliot has reminded us that a great writer is not only a master of language, he is also its servant, and language, in Coleridge's words, is 'the embodied and articulated spirit of the Race', 'a magnificent History of acts of individual minds, sanctioned by the collective Mind of the Country'[1]; in using language creatively the writer invokes—in part deliberately, in part intuitively and unconsciously—the accumulated thought and experience that has shaped it.[2] It is the same with the writer's more or less deliberate use of symbols of recognized significance and power. These very obviously have a context, and what makes for success in any instance is not only the particular operation of the artist's genius but the availability of a tradition. I speak with diffidence here, but I take it that what is weak in *Moby Dick*—among so much that is strong—may be partly explained by the absence of a coherent body of symbols and a tradition of symbolic thinking such as were available to Dante

---

[1] T. S. Eliot, *Selected Prose,* ed. John Hayward (Pelican), p. 100; Coleridge, *Aids to Reflection,* ed. Thomas Fenby (1896), p. 212; autograph notebook, quoted by A. D. Snyder, *Coleridge on Logic and Learning,* p. 138. ('A man of genius using a rich and expressive language (the Greek, German, or English) is an excellent instance and illustration of the ever individualizing process and dynamic Being of Ideas. What a magnificent History of acts of individual minds, sanctioned by the collective Mind of the Country, a Language is.')

[2] As Professor Vinaver says of Racine's language in a passage that is very relevant in the present connexion, 'Words have poetic life only in so far as they condense their own history'.—*Racine and Poetic Tragedy* (translated by P. Mansell Jones), p. 78. See Owen Barfield, *Poetic Diction.* It is hardly necessary to add that the writer's genius also shows itself in *keeping out* irrelevant or incongruous associations.

in the thirteenth century.[1] When there is a rich tradition of that kind the meanings of a writer who uses the symbols necessarily include a reference to the tradition, which is itself part of the relevant context, even though clearly enough it cannot do the writer's work for him.

All this is familiar ground. What needs to be brought out however is that 'context' even as so far used—the context within which the writer defines his symbols—is not, from the reader's point of view, something simply given, fixed, static, and belonging solely to a past which he picks over to glean information. As with all aspects of literature, for the defining context to be effective there is necessary not only the art of the writer but also the collaborative activity of the reader. As Professor Walsh puts it:

> Words are not formulae. Scientific symbols are engaged almost exclusively in pointing beyond themselves, they neither require nor reward involvement, they are thoroughly bleached of everything but reference. Words as symbols, on the other hand, always contain more than reference; what they point to is also in part embodied in and enacted by them, and they compel in consequence some degree of involvement.[2]

In other words there is a *forward-looking* element—the ability to assimilate and use—in the very act of understanding what any particular symbol may mean. And although this is true of the understanding of *any* expression, whether symbolic or not—for all understanding involves the power to use and deploy in

---

[1] For the break with an older tradition, as well as the persistence and renewal of some forms of symbolic thinking in nineteenth-century America, see Charles Feidelson, Jr., *Symbolism and American Literature*. H. Flanders Dunbar deals at length with the inherited tradition of the age of Dante in *Symbolism in Medieval Thought and its Consummation in the Divine Comedy*. In *A Reading of George Herbert*, Rosemond Tuve deals with the availability of a tradition of symbolic thinking in the early seventeenth century.

[2] William Walsh, 'Theory of Language and Practice in Education, and T. S. Eliot', *The Use of Imagination: Educational Thought and the Literary Mind*, p. 238. See also p. 242.

fresh circumstances what is communicated[1]—the mere range
of reference of 'symbolic' writing ensures that the activity of
understanding shall be correspondingly strong and ranging.

The fact is however that our response to expressive or imaginative symbols goes far beyond 'understanding', if by that we
mean some kind of detached knowledge in which the reader is
not essentially involved. Poetry for example can be regarded as
a rather complicated language game of which the rules can be
learnt by an acute mind. But to read poetry in this way is
obviously to denature it: our response to even the simplest lyric
is something very different from the response, 'Why, yes, I see
how it works', or even, 'How interesting!' As Maritain says,

> The fact remains, in any case, that not only those who glancing
> at a work expect from it a mere pleasurable mirroring of their
> own customary feelings, habits of thought and trite perceptiveness
> simply live in barbarous parts, but also that a mere external
> contemplation of a work, appreciating its qualities even with
> trained intelligence and aesthetic discernment, but from the
> outside, remains on the threshold of poetry. We must listen to
> the interiority of the work and to the poetic sense, be open to
> what it conveys, let ourselves be attracted by the magnetic ring
> of which Plato spoke. And this requires a sort of previous,
> tentative *cons nt*—to the work and to the intentions of the poet—
> without which we cannot be taken into the confidence of the
> poem.[2]

This seems to me true of all art, but it applies with especial force
to those powerful nuclei of meanings for which we find ourselves using the word 'symbol'. A symbol, I have said, takes its
meaning from a context: but—as it were—overlapping with
the given context is the context of each individual's developing

---

[1] This point is put effectively by Professor H. H. Price in *Thinking and
Experience* (pp. 230–1)—a book, it should be said here, which illuminates
many aspects of image-thinking.

[2] Jacques Maritain, *Creative Intuition in Art and Poetry*, p. 308.

life experience, and the full meaning—the generative power—only exists in so far as this too is in some way, powerfully or subtly, affected.

That, I suppose, is most obvious with regard to the symbols and symbolic events of religion. Certainly these can be studied, as material for psychology, anthropology, the history of religions, and so on. But as operative symbols they only exist for the kind of knowledge that is also an involvement.[1]

Erich Auerbach, in the first chapter of his book, *Mimesis*, makes an impressive contrast between an episode in the *Odyssey* and the Old Testament story of the sacrifice of Isaac (Genesis 22).[2] His point is that in the Homeric narrative there is no 'background', only 'foreground': 'What [Homer] narrates is for the time being the only present, and fills both the stage and the reader's mind completely' (p. 4). 'Such a problematic psychological situation [as that of Abraham commanded to sacrifice Isaac] is impossible for any of the Homeric heroes, whose destiny is clearly defined and who wake every morning as though it were the first day of their lives' (p. 12). In the Biblical story, on the other hand (and in this it is characteristic of the Old Testament narratives), we are conscious of a history that presses on the present moment, much that is of the greatest importance is left unsaid, depths of meaning are implied; 'the whole ... remains mysterious and "fraught with background"' (pp. 11–12). This applies to the separate personages as well as to events.

God is always so represented in the Bible, for he is not comprehensible in his presence, as is Zeus; it is always only 'something' of him that appears, he always extends into depths. But even the

[1] There are of course degrees of involvement. Full commitment to the major symbols of any religion involves a profession of belief. But it is also clear that very many religious symbols are operative outside the bounds of the religion to which in a special sense they belong.

[2] Erich Auerbach, *Mimesis: The Representation of Reality in Western Literature* (translated by Williard R. Trask), Chapter I, 'Odysseus' Scar'.

human beings in the Biblical stories have greater depths of time, fate and consciousness than do the human beings in Homer; although they are nearly always caught up in an event engaging all their faculties, they are not so entirely immersed in its present that they do not remain continually conscious of what has happened to them earlier and elsewhere; their thoughts and feelings have more layers, are more entangled. Abraham's actions are explained not only by what is happening to him at the moment, nor yet only by his character . . . , but by his previous history; he remembers, he is constantly conscious of, what God has promised him and what God has already accomplished for him—his soul is torn between desperate rebellion and hopeful expectation; his silent obedience is multilayered, has background (p. 12).

A consequence of this is that whereas 'Homer can be analysed . . . but he cannot be interpreted' (p. 13), the Abraham–Isaac story *demands* interpretation. 'Since so much in the story is dark and incomplete, and since the reader knows that God is a hidden God, his effort to interpret it constantly finds something new to feed upon' (p. 15). Moreover, the Biblical narrative claims 'absolute authority'. 'Far from seeking . . . merely to make us forget our own reality for a few hours, it seeks to overcome our reality: we are to fit our own life into its world, feel ourselves to be elements in its structure of universal history' (p. 15).

This is a bald summary of an essay of which the impressiveness lies largely in the detailed analysis, but it may be held to establish a point of the greatest importance in the present connexion. The sacrifice of Isaac is a symbol in the Coleridgean sense—it 'partakes of the reality which it renders intelligible'; whilst remaining a moving story, firmly anchored to the actual, it 'demands' interpretation—demands it, that is, by the very manner of its telling, by the kind of claim it makes on the reader, and for the sake of the meaning that we sense within it. And interpretation obviously is something very different from the skilful manipulation of other events around the story which

may illuminate it: it is essentially an inward process in which
we can only hope for understanding to the extent that our own
experience—at different levels of consciousness—is brought to
a focus in the symbolic structure: self and story are mutually
illuminating.[1] Paul Tillich, speaking of religious language, but
with an awareness of similar processes in poetry and the other
arts, says:

> Every symbol opens up a level of reality for which non-symbolic
> speaking is inadequate. . . . But in order to do this, something
> else must be opened up—namely, levels of the soul, levels of our
> interior reality. And they must correspond to the levels in exterior
> reality which are opened up by a symbol. So every symbol is
> two-edged. It opens up reality and it opens up the soul.[2]

George Herbert put the same idea, perhaps more simply, when,
in a poem addressed to the Bible, he wrote:

> Such are thy secrets, which my life makes good,
>   And comments on thee; for in ev'ry thing
>   Thy words do find me out, and parallels bring,
> And in another make me understood.[3]

[1] 'Self' of course includes sub-conscious drives. For the psycho-analytic
implications of the story and its relevance to relationships within the
family, see *Isaac and Oedipus*, by Erich Wellesch.

[2] Paul Tillich, *Theology of Culture*, 'The Nature of Religious Language',
pp. 56–7. Cf. Ronald W. Hepburn, 'Poetry and Religious Belief', in *Metaphysical Beliefs*, ed. A. C. MacIntyre, p. 142: 'The power of meditative verse
such as Herbert's is largely due to its making the reader feel that the Biblical
types are not only being restated but also that their creative life is still
producing new enrichment of its own materials, new startling transformations of the familiar, the seemingly "tamed" and archaic. He feels also that
he is *participating* in the life of the symbols; his own life is caught up in
theirs; he is not the mere spectator of an exegetical exercise.' And Coleridge:
'This, then, is the prerogative of the Bible; this is the privilege of its believing
students. With them the principle of knowledge is likewise a spring and
principle of action.'—*The Statesman's Manual* (in White, *Political Tracts of
Wordsworth etc.*), p. 19.

[3] 'The Holy Scriptures, ii.'

The truth of this, as applied to the symbols of religion, would, I think, be generally admitted. What seems to be less generally recognized is that it applies also to the symbols of the poets. It is the principle of involvement, of some degree of personal commitment, *that makes symbols*. It is easy to be misunderstood on this point, and I should like to make it clear that I do not regard a tensed desire for self-improvement as a suitable attitude in which to read poetry; neither do I regard a life devoted to literature as a series of moral crises. I am referring to the supple and subtle life of the mind when it is wholly engaged in an imaginative act. 'The whole soul of man' which the poet 'brings into activity'[1] includes not only perception, feeling and judgment, but motions of assent which, if too slight to be regarded as conscious will, are nevertheless the ground from which emerges an orientation to life as a whole.

Three short examples may help us here.

You never Enjoy the World aright, till the Sea it self floweth in your Veins, till you are Clothed with the Heavens, and Crowned with the Stars. . . . (Traherne, *Centuries of Meditation*, I, 29)

Man is all symmetry,
Full of proportions, one limb to another,
And all to all the world besides:
Each part may call the furthest, brother:
For head with foot hath private amity,
And both with moons and tides.

(George Herbert, 'Man')

. . . when you do dance, I wish you
A wave o' the sea, that you might ever do
Nothing but that; move still, still so,
And own no other function . . .

(Shakespeare, *The Winter's Tale*, IV, iv)

[1] *Biographia Literaria* (ed. Shawcross), Vol. II, p. 12.

I am not sure what an intelligent scientist who read little poetry would make of these. The Shakespeare might pass as a graceful compliment to a girl. The Herbert might be found interesting as an expression of something no longer believed in—for example, the notion that different parts of the body were affected by the motion of moon and stars and planets. The Traherne would probably be regarded as, at most, vaguely 'poetical'. Well of course Florizel's lines to Perdita are a graceful compliment. What more they are the poetry enforces. Not only is the rhythm of the waves evoked, together with the speaker's responsive delight, in the firm and delicate rhythm of the lines; the action of the human dancer is related—by something more than an illustrative analogy—to the impersonal movement of the sea. Once that is recognized the still living import of the lines from Herbert and Traherne—so far from mere quaintness or mere 'poetry'—comes into view. What all three passages have in common is not only a deep responsiveness to the great natural rhythms; implicit in the Herbert and Traherne, virtually explicit in the Shakespeare, is a sense of the impersonal depths of the personality. None of these poets could have written as he did unless he had felt that the conscious ego rests on, draws its strength from, something greater than itself. No one can 'understand' their lines unless he meets them with a corresponding recognition that is also an affirmation. It may well not appear as a conscious affirmation—indeed anything approaching that would run the risk of slipping over into sentimentality; it may only appear as delight. But it is only when the roots of the will are touched that the meaning of the sea symbolism appears. Even so delicate and slight an attunement as we make in responding to the rhythm of George Herbert's lines—

> For head with foot hath private amity,
> And both with moons and tides—

belongs to the same world—the world of action and relationship and commitment—as that in which we make and enact our being. And so, as Henry James said in a different connexion, 'among our innumerable acts, are no arbitrary, no senseless separations. The more we are capable of acting the less gropingly we plead such differences; whereby, with any capability, we recognize betimes that to "put" things is very exactly and responsibly and interminably to do them. Our expression of them, and the terms on which we understand that, belong as nearly to our conduct and our life as every other feature of our freedom.'[1]

I think that instances of the kind just given could be multiplied, and that examination of them would likewise lead us to a position diametrically opposed to that implied in an assertion Susanne Langer once made, 'Art . . . has no consequences.'[2] For the symbol, at all events, to have consequences is an integral part of the meaning. For Coleridge (since we are still working within the field of his promptings) the apprehension of a symbol is clearly an imaginative act; and if there is one attribute above all others, that, throughout his critical writings, Coleridge assigns to the imagination it is that of a transforming *energy* of the mind. To the other union of opposites in the symbol—the 'translucence' of the special in the individual, of the whole in the part, of the eternal in the temporal—we may add the active involvement of the self—the whole self—in the self-forgetful act of contemplation. 'Yet consider', Coleridge said, 'that like can only be known by like: that as truth is the correlative of being, so is the act of being the great organ of truth: that in natural no less than in moral science, *quantum sumus, scimus*.'[3]

I hope that this has helped to make sense of my earlier state-

[1] Preface to the *The Golden Bowl*, p. xxviii.
[2] *Philosophy in a New Key* (Mentor Books), p. 214.
[3] *The Statesman's Manual*, p. 39. On the relation between idea and symbol, reason and imagination, in Coleridge, see D. G. James, 'The Thought of Coleridge', in *The Major English Romantic Poets*, edited by Clarence D. Thorpe, Carlos Baker and Bennett Weaver.

ment that the meaning of a literary symbol emerges from two interlocking contexts, that of the created work (including the more or less that it brings into play from tradition) and that of the reader's own life in the very process of living. Because of this the symbol is both 'tied' and 'free'. It is tied by the artist's power to integrate all elements of meaning in a closely articulated structure: you can't make Blake's sick rose or Dante's *selva oscura* mean just anything you choose. It is free because the meaning has not been given once for all, it develops and takes on substance as it 'opens up' 'levels of our interior reality' and becomes incorporated in our being. Like the Coleridgean idea (and we have seen how closely Coleridge associated idea and symbol) it is 'living, productive, partakes of infinity . . . and contains an endless power of semination'.[1] What we have to do with, therefore, is no paraphrasable meaning but a direction of the personality as a whole.[2] It is the capacity of symbols (both individual symbols and whole imaginative works in their symbolic aspect) to foster a life-direction that explains our sense of the very great importance of the kind of inquiry undertaken in this Symposium. What is in question is nothing less than a fundamental quality of human life—man's capacity for growth and renewal in response to the transforming energies in structures of the imagination.

> For out of olde feldes, as men seyth,
> Cometh al this newe corn from yer to yere.

[1] See *The Statesman's Manual*, pp. 21–2.

[2] We must of course guard against the implication that this is only—or even usually—a matter of conscious will. The direction springs from a preparedness to live one's life in a certain way, and this includes an openness to promptings from below the threshold of consciousness. 'One must be able to *let things happen*. I have learned from the East what it means by the phrase "Wu wei": namely not-doing, letting be, which is quite different from doing nothing. Some Occidentals, also, have known what this not-doing means; for instance, Meister Eckhardt, who speaks of "sich lassen", to let oneself be.'—Jung, *The Integration of the Personality* (English edition, 1940), pp. 31–2.

Perhaps it should be added that to seek the meaning of a symbol in a direction, a state of being, rather than in any analysable propositions, however subtle, is not to express a preference for 'floating and obscure generalities'.[1] When Coleridge spoke of 'ideas which may indeed be suggested and awakened, but cannot, like the images of sense and the conceptions of the understanding, be adequately expressed by words',[2] he was not turning his back on his life-long plea for habits of mental accuracy and verbal precision; he was merely reminding us that our habits of thought must be adequate to the material with which they profess to deal.

[1] Coleridge, *Essays on his Own Times*, Vol. II, p. 543.
[2] *Church and State*, p. 176.

King Lear as Metaphor

I HAD better begin by saying that I am not altogether happy about the title I have chosen for this paper. 'Metaphor', like 'myth' and 'archetype', is in danger of becoming an incantatory word; and I must confess that if anyone were to ask me for a short definition of 'a metaphor', I should find myself hard pressed for an answer. My purpose, however, is not incantation but inquiry, and it seems to me that to apply such knowledge as we have of metaphoric working to *King Lear* may throw light on a problem raised not only by *King Lear* but by all works of literary art.

The problem I have in mind concerns the perpetually renewed meaning of any poem (and the sense I intend would include many works in prose: *Wuthering Heights*, for example, and *The Castle*, and *A Passage to India*). The greater the poem the more obvious it is that the meaning—unlike, say, a theorem in geometry—is not given once and for all, but that it includes the capacity for change and renewal. Harold Goddard, in 'A Word to the Reader' which prefaces his fine book, *The Meaning of Shakespeare*, puts well what I have in mind:

> That Shakespeare is primarily a poet ought to be so obvious that even to put the thought in words would be banal. That it is not only not banal but is the thing most necessary to emphasize about him at the present time is a comment on the long ascendancy of the historical school of criticism in Shakespeare study. In stressing what Shakespeare meant to the Elizabethan age the historical critics have helped us forget what he might mean to ours. Like the materialists of the nineteenth century, in focusing attention on where things come from they tend to forget where they are going. They tend to forget that poetry means creation, and creation is something that still goes on.[1]

[1] Harold Goddard, *The Meaning of Shakespeare* (Phoenix Books, University of Chicago Press), Vol. I, pp. viii–ix.

'Poetry', as Goddard says later in the same book, 'forever makes itself over for each generation': and I think it is plain not only that *King Lear* meant something different to Dr Johnson from what it means to any twentieth-century reader, but that it must mean something different for each reader, even of the same generation, who has genuinely entered into the play and made it his own. That is one side of the problem. But it is also true that the meaning of *King Lear* is not simply subjective, a matter of individual taste or fancy. Confronted by the poem you are certainly not at liberty to read into it anything you choose. Indeed the whole business of criticism, of the intelligent discussion of literature, presupposes that there is sound sense in Matthew Arnold's statement of the function of criticism, 'To see the object as in itself it really is'. The only way to reconcile these apparently contradictory truths it seems to me, is through an examination of the nature of metaphor and the metaphoric process.

At this point I propose to invoke the help of Martin Foss in that difficult but far-reaching and seminal book, *Symbol and Metaphor in Human Experience*.[1] Foss is concerned not with literary criticism in any limited sense but with ways of representing life, and therefore of living it. His argument is based on the distinction between the pursuit of 'ends' determined by the will (and therefore conceived in terms of what is fixed and static) and the acceptance of a 'direction'; between the closed world of the consistent empiricist and the 'open' (but not lawless) world of creative living. It is to the former of these two worlds that Foss rather arbitrarily and contrary to most current usage, assigns the symbol. (That for Foss's 'symbol' most of us would prefer to use the word 'sign' is, for the moment, irrelevant.) The symbol is a fixed representation of the empirical world: 'clear, exact and useful' (p. 3), it belongs to the 'purposive, constructed environ-

[1] Martin Foss, *Symbol and Metaphor in Human Experience* (Bison Book edition, University of Nebraska Press).

ment of the ego with all its deeds and fulfilments' (p. 131). To the symbolic reduction (subsuming manifold variety under a fixed representation) Foss opposes the metaphoric process: 'metaphors break up instead of fixing, keep us on the move instead of letting us settle down' (p. 58). Over against the symbolic world of 'similarity, comparison and repetition' (p. 89) is 'metaphorical life with its seeming contradictions, tensions, and its transcendence' (p. 87). 'Metaphor is a process of tension and energy, manifested in the process of language, not in the single word' (p. 61).[1]

It is the idea of process that is important, for what we have to do with is something that goes far beyond the concept of metaphor as an isolated figure of speech in which, as the dictionary says, 'a term or phrase is applied to something to which it is not literally applicable in order to suggest a resemblance'. It is a process in which terms representing items of our knowledge are brought into relation to each other and to something unknown; and in a mutual interaction (for even the unknown is felt like the tug of a current or tide) fixed meanings are modified or destroyed, and a new apprehension—or (shall we say?) a new direction of awareness—takes place. What Foss is describing is of course *the* creative movement of all literary form, from the highest poetry to the humblest expression of an intuitive awareness such as the proverb. Indeed what Foss says of the proverb will serve as a convenient summary of his thinking about the metaphoric process in its widest manifestations:

A proverb may appear as a simile, a comparison, but it is very different. The comparison connects one object with another in order to procure additional knowledge. But if we take a proverb like 'Among blind men the one-eyed is king', we may consider

[1] For the 'tensive' quality of creative metaphor and some criticism of Foss, see Philip Wheelwright, *The Burning Fountain: A Study in the Language of Symbolism* (Indiana University Press), Chapter VI, and *Metaphor and Reality* (Indiana University Press).

it as a comparison between two groups, the blind and the seeing. If we, however, learn only what the simile tells us: that the one-eyed can be compared to a king when he lives among blind men, then the result of our comparison is rather foolish. In fact, neither the one-eyed man nor the king is the real interest, neither of the two is supposed to profit by the comparison. The true significance of the proverb goes far beyond the blind, the one-eyed, and the king: it points to a wisdom in regard to which the terms of the comparison are only unimportant cases of reference. It teaches the relativity and deficiency of all wordly power, and this wisdom, without being expressly stated, rises above the transient analogy and its inadequate formula. It lifts us above these and other cases of an arbitrary selection to a lawful necessity. Although the form of the proverb is still very much like the simile, even like the riddle, witty and surprising, playfully enclosing a general rule into the nutshell of particular cases, nevertheless its transcending character points to the metaphoric sphere. For it may now be stated: the simile and the analogy link the unknown to the known, in an expedient and practical way, closing the problematic entity into a familiar pattern. The meta-phorical process, on the contrary, raises the problem even there where we seemed at home and shatters the ground on which we had settled down in order to widen our view beyond any limit of a special practical use. (pp. 55-56)

The metaphoric process, thus defined, is therefore the central drive of all literary creation (the making of a living image of experience that goes beyond the immediate representation), but more marked and explicit as the work approaches great poetry. There are many works of literature (e.g. realistic novels) where the metaphoric element is comparatively slight. There are others where to ignore or misunderstand the metaphoric working is to be left with but a meagre skeleton of the living experience that is offered in, for example, poetic drama. In a work almost wholly metaphorical a mind unsympathetic to this mode of understanding will be completely baffled and will find, not reason in its

172

most exalted mood, but plain nonsense. A German critic once dismissed *King Lear* as 'a nursery story, but of the more horrible sort'. But the most eminent representative of this way of mistaking things is Tolstoy, whose remarks on *King Lear*, in the essay, 'Shakespeare and the Drama',[1] may serve to close this introductory section and lead us into some consideration of the play itself.

Tolstoy's conception of the function of art led him to claim that the aim of drama is 'to elicit sympathy with what is represented' (p. 353). For this, illusion—'which constitutes the chief condition of art' (p. 336)—is essential, and the context makes plain that what Tolstoy meant by illusion was an imaginative sympathy or identification with the *dramatis personae* as though they were characters in a real-life situation.

> An artistic poetic work, especially a drama, should first of all evoke in reader or spectator the illusion that what the persons represented are living through and experiencing is being lived through and experienced by himself. . . . However eloquent and profound they may be, speeches put into the mouths of acting characters, if they are superfluous and do not accord with the situation and the characters, infringe the main condition of dramatic work—the illusion causing the reader or spectator to experience the feelings of the persons represented. One may without infringing the illusion leave much unsaid: the reader or spectator will himself supply what is needed . . .; but to say what is superfluous, is like jerking and scattering a statue made up of small pieces, or taking the lamp out of a magic lantern . . . the illusion is lost, and to recreate it is sometimes impossible. (p. 354)

We may leave on one side for the moment the question of what is or is not superfluous and who is the best judge of this (for to determine what is superfluous means that one already has a conception of what is proper): it is plain that what Tolstoy demands

---

[1] Included in the World's Classics volume, *Recollections and Essays*, translated with an Introduction by Aylmer Maude. Page references are to this volume.

is a straightforward verisimilitude to life. With such a criterion he has no difficulty in showing (though he does it at some length) that *King Lear* is arbitrary, unnatural, and ridiculous. Mr Wilson Knight, in a valuable paper,[1] claims that Tolstoy's powerful mind was misled by the nineteenth-century commentators on Shakespeare, with their excessive emphasis on 'character': Tolstoy was perplexed because he expected, and did not find, in Shakespeare 'the novelist's skill, tending more towards "observation" and "imitation" ' than towards those poetic and symbolic forms through which Shakespeare bodies forth 'a central dynamic idea'. Not finding what he had been led to expect, he was baffled and angry and inclined to shout humbug at those who admire. What also has to be said (I think it is implied in Mr Wilson Knight's analysis) is that Tolstoy seems to think that for the purpose of critical demonstration a prose paraphrase and summary will do as well as the original poetry, which is essentially metaphoric.

There is no need to do more than remind you of how far, in *King Lear*, Shakespeare is from concerning himself with naturalistic illusion. Not only are there bold improbabilities (the parallel plots, Edgar's disguises, Dover cliff, etc.), there is an almost complete rejection of verisimilitude in the portrayal of the characters and their setting, of anything that might seem to keep us in close touch with a familiar—or at all events an actual—world. This, as I say, is now commonplace, but a rather obvious contrast may be useful here. The first chapter of Turgenev's novel, *A King Lear of the Steppe*, opens with a long description of the hero, Kharlov:

Imagine a man of gigantic height. On his huge torso rested, a little aslant and without any sign of a neck, an enormous head; a whole shock of tangled yellow-gray hair rose up from it, starting practically from his ruffled eyebrows themselves. On the broad

[1] G. Wilson Knight, *Shakespeare and Tolstoy*, The English Association, Pamphlet No. 88.

square of his dove-coloured face there stuck out a big, knobby
nose; his tiny little light blue eyes puffed out arrogantly, and his
mouth hung open—also tiny, but crooked, chapped, and the
same colour as the rest of his face. The voice that came out of this
mouth was, though husky, extremely strong and stentorian. Its
sound reminded you of the clanking of flat iron bars in a cart on
a rough pavement, and Kharlov would talk as if shouting to someone across a wide ravine in a strong wind.[1]

Solidity of specification is the keynote, and Turgenev took
great pains to ensure that characters and setting alike should
seem to have an historical existence in a particular bit of Russia
in the first half of the nineteenth century. 'Technical information—for example, the procedures connected with the division
of the estate between the two daughters, or the correct names
of the beams and rafters in a roof—[he] asked of his friends,
acquaintances, and the steward of his own estate.'[2] Much of
the success of the story depends on what Mr Franklin Reeve
calls the 'accuracy and actualness of the incidents [Turgenev]
imagined his characters tied to'.

By contrast, what do we know of Lear's appearance, or of
what the heath looked like? Lear is a powerful old man, 'four
score and upward', and the crown of his head ('this thin helm')
is covered by a few white hairs; the heath is a desolate place
('For many miles about there's scarce a bush'): that is all we
know of the appearance of either. And just as specificness of
person and setting is a main feature of Turgenev's novel, so the
rejection of it is characteristic of Shakespeare's tragedy.[3] A. C.

---

[1] Turgenev, *Five Short Novels*, translated and with an Introduction by
Franklin Reeve (New York: Bantam Books).
[2] Franklin Reeve, Preface to *A King Lear of the Steppe*. The following
quotation is from the same source.
[3] On the stage of course the characters 'look like' the actors who play
their roles, but Shakespeare has provided indications enough that these
should be, so far as possible, depersonalized: individualizing gestures and
mannerisms should be at all costs avoided.

Bradley rightly speaks of 'the vagueness of the scene where the action takes place, and of the movements of the figures which cross this scene; the strange atmosphere, cold and dark, which strikes on us as we enter this scene, enfolding these figures and magnifying their dim outlines like a winter mist.'[1] Granville-Barker speaks of 'a certain megalithic grandeur . . . that we associate with Greek tragedy.'[2]

What this means is that a certain simplification of effect is an essential part of Shakespeare's method in *King Lear*. Ignoring for the moment the important conversation between Gloucester and Kent with which the play opens, we see that the first scene turns on a situation reduced to its bare essentials. It is of course the love-test that puts before us the central conflict in Lear— an old man who wants the prerogatives of age, but combined with the privileged treatment appropriate to babyhood; a king who wants power, but without responsibility; a father who wants love, but seeks to treat it as though it were some kind of commodity that could be bought or enforced. Since this sort of things happens every day, I do not see how anyone can speak of the scene as 'unnatural'. But obviously it is not presented naturalistically: Granville-Barker speaks of 'the almost ritual formality of the first scene', and the formal quality is enforced not only by the starkness with which the issues are presented but by such devices as the use of rhymed couplets (instead of the more 'natural' prose or blank verse) at crucial points. Now the 'stripping' of character and situation, aided by a certain formality in the presentation, has, as the play develops, a curious effect. Instead of a simple sparseness (as in a morality play like *Everyman*)

[1] *Shakespearean Tragedy*, p. 247. Bradley feels the effect of this, even though he curiously complains that it 'interferes with dramatic clearness even when the play is read'.

[2] H. Granville-Barker, *Prefaces to Shakespeare*, First Series, p. 146. Granville-Barker quotes the passage from Bradley when answering the latter's contention that *Lear*, although 'Shakespeare's greatest achievement', is '*not* his best play'.

there is an almost overwhelming richness. Boundaries are firmly
drawn: certain interests are excluded, and there are questions we
are not allowed to ask. But this simplification is the condition of
the greatest possible compression and intensification: character
and situation alike take on a symbolic quality and are made to
point to a range of experience beyond themselves. And they do
this because of the ways in which the reader or spectator is
involved in the metaphoric process that constitutes the play.

From the start *King Lear* sets you asking questions, and not
only obvious and inescapable ones such as, Why has Lear staged
this curious love-test in conjunction with the division of his
kingdom? or, Is Cordelia right or wrong in refusing to humour
her father? The questions we are made to ask are of a particular
kind. Tolstoy sometimes makes it a matter of complaint that
Shakespeare leaves us without explanations even when it would
be easy to provide them;[1] but that is just where Tolstoy mistakes
the nature of Shakespearean drama. The questions raised by
King Lear do not allow 'explanations' that you can complacently
store in a pocket of the mind: they seem designed to cause the
greatest possible uncertainty, or even bewilderment. Within
the areas cleared by a formal simplification they centre on certain words and conceptions: in the first scene, 'love' and
'nothing' and 'unnatural' (shortly to be joined by 'Nature'),
and then as the play proceeds, 'fool' and 'need'.

Now all of these words are profoundly ambiguous. Let us
glance in passing at 'nothing', recalling as do so the unexpectedly
wise words of Richard II in his dungeon:

> Nor I, nor anyone that but man is,
> With nothing shall be pleased, till he be eased
> With being nothing.

What this says is that no man will be content with mere depriva-
tion until he is dead and so past caring; but simultaneously it has

[1] See 'Shakespeare and the Drama', *Recollections and Essays*, p. 346.

the effect of suggesting that all men are pleased with vanities ('nothings') until they are either physically dead or in some sense dead to the world. There is a simple ambiguousness in the 'nothing' that plays between Lear and Cordelia.

> Lear.   Now, our joy,
>   Although our last, not least; to whose young love
>   The vines of France and milk of Burgundy
>   Strive to be interess'd; what can you say to draw
>   A third more opulent than your sisters? Speak.
> Cordelia. Nothing, my lord.
> Lear.   Nothing?
> Cordelia. Nothing.
> Lear.   Nothing will come of nothing: speak again.

'Nothing': on the one hand mere negation, the absence of what is desired ('Can you make no use of nothing, Nuncle?' 'Why, no, boy; nothing can be made out of nothing.'); on the other hand, the possession of the inestimable, which the world does not regard.

> Fairest Cordelia, that art most rich, being poor;
> Most choice, forsaken; and most lov'd despis'd!

With these lines Richmond Noble compares 2 Corinthians vi, 10: 'As poor, and yet making many rich: as having nothing, and yet possessing all things.'[1]

It is the same with all our key-words, and I should like for a moment to present you with a ridiculously abstract description of their working. (1) The key-words—words to which special attention is directed—are all ambiguous and cover a wide range of meaning. (2) Poetry and situation release and bring into relation and conflict the different meanings: the words, in

---

[1] Richmond Noble, *Shakespeare's Biblical Knowledge*, p. 229, quoted by Kenneth Muir in a note to the New Arden edition. The section on Lear's Fool in Miss Enid Welsford's *The Fool: his Social and Literary History* is very relevant at this point.

Empson's phrase, are 'complex words'.[1] (3) So great is the activation of these words, instance piled on instance in quick succession, that they vibrate in the reader's mind beyond the limits of the specific instances. When within a space easily encompassed by the mind in one act of apprehension we have fire and whirlpool, bog and quagmire, whirlwinds and star-blasting, the web and the pin (cataract), squint-eyes, hare-lip and mildewed wheat, then our sense of natural calamity stretches on and on: behind the whirlpool is all shipwreck, behind the mildewed wheat is all failure of harvest and starvation.[2] (4) Just as there is interplay and tension between the different senses of the key-words, so there is interplay and tension between the different key-words themselves and all the other elements of the drama.

As a way of drawing to a point these observations, let us follow the course of one such key-word, arbitrarily disengaging it from the others. It is not, as it happens, mentioned in the opening scenes where the situation to be elucidated is set forth.[3] But it lies behind both the first scene, where Lear makes his test and divides his kingdom, and the second, where the parallel and intensifying plot is got under way. The word is Justice. Both Lear and Edmund are concerned for some form—a perverted form—of distributive justice. Lear is concerned that reward should be proportioned to merit, that is, the merit of proclaimed love to him ('That we our largest bounty may extend/Where nature doth with merit challenge'); Edmund is concerned with the unfair social discrimination in favour of legitimate sons and

[1] William Empson, *The Structure of Complex Words*.

[2] The effect is analogous to the effect of the sub-plot as described in W. B. Yeats' essay, 'The Emotion of Multitude', in *Ideas of Good and Evil; Essays and Introductions*, pp. 215–16.

[3] 'The distinctive Shakespearean structure comes, not so much from the need to compress a series of events within the framework of a play, but rather from a powerful urge to elucidate, and even exhaust, the meaning of the opening situation.'—L. A. Cormican, 'Medieval Idiom in Shakespeare', *Scrutiny*, XVII, 3–4.

the hardships of primogeniture, for both of which he would substitute the criterion of a particular kind of desert: 'To each', he seems to say, 'according to his ability to get'—'All with me's meet that I can fashion fit'. Lear's perfomance has even something of the appearance of a formal trial, just as trial procedure will appear again when Lear arraigns Goneril and Regan before the Bedlam and the Fool, and when Cornwall acts as accuser, judge and executioner in a summary trial for 'treason'. Legal or quasi-legal procedure is in fact enacted or referred to a good many times in the play: Kent is put in the stocks, Poor Tom has been 'whipp'd from tithing to tithing, and stock-punished, and imprison'd', and Edgar and Edmund engage in judicial combat; there are references to unfee'd lawyers, summoners, cases in law, beadles, hanging and the rack. All this is sufficient to raise some question about the nature of justice, even without the play's explicit insistence at crucial points.

To the question, What is Justice? the play offers many answers, more or less adequate. The commonest assumption of the characters is that it is some kind of assignment of reward or punishment according to desert, and their human assumptions are often projected on to 'the gods'.

> Let the great Gods,
> That keep this dreadful pudder o'er our heads,
> Find out their enemies now. Tremble, thou wretch,
> That hast within thee undivulged crimes,
> Unwhipp'd of Justice; hide thee, thou bloody hand,
> Thou perjur'd, and thou simular of virtue
> That art incestuous; caitiff, to pieces shake,
> That under covert and convenient seeming
> Hast practis'd on man's life: close pent-up guilts
> Rive your concealing continents, and cry
> These dreadful summoners grace.

'Unwhipp'd of Justice'; beind that conception of justice lies Lear's own vindictive desire to 'punish home' for offences against

himself. Its inadequacy is underlined by the play's two references to legal whipping: the lunatic beggar is 'whipp'd from
tithing to tithing' simply because he is a vagabond; the prosti-
tute is lashed by the parish beadle whose cruelty is fed by his lust.

Distributive and retributive justice alike assume that man can
determine degrees of desert and merit on a calculated scale.
What the play tells you is that he can't. There is indeed a justice
in the grain of things—something like, I suppose, the Greek
dîke—in the sense that there is an inner logic of events whereby
evil consumes itself: Albany's

> This shows you are above,
> You justicers, that these our nether crimes
> So speedily can venge.

But the merely human assignment of guilt and punishment,
desert and reward (mixed as this assignment is with unacknowledged and distorting passions), is shown to have no ultimate
justification at all: in the play's total vision there seems little
difference between the claim of the lawless individualist to assert
his own version of nature's law and socially sanctioned legal
forms. The *reductio ad absurdum* of Lear's view of his own role
as dispenser of justice is of course the mock trial of Goneril
and Regan.

Lear. I'll see their trial first. Bring in their evidence.
    [*To Edgar*] Thou robed man of justice, take thy place;
    [*To the Fool*] And thou, his yoke-fellow of equity,
    Bench by his side. [*To Kent*] You are o'th' commission,
    Sit you too.
Edgar. Let us deal justly. . . .
    Purr, the cat is grey.
Lear. Arraign her first; 'tis Goneril. I here take my oath before
    this honourable assembly, she kick'd the poor King her
    father.
Fool. Come hither, mistress. Is your name Goneril?
Lear. She cannot deny it.

Fool.   Cry you mercy, I took you for a joint-stool.
Lear.   And here's another, whose warp'd looks proclaim
        What store her heart is made on. Stop her there!
        Arms, arms, sword, fire! Corruption in the place!
        False justicer, why hast thou let her 'scape?

If I may quote what I have said elsewhere, there is ' "corruption
in the place" indeed. Lear's fantasy spins right when, by bringing
the trial to an end in mad confusion, it tells him that reality
cannot be reached in that way'.[1] This, and much else, lies behind
Lear's great explicit denunciation—'reason in madness'—of
human authority and its legalistic claims.

Lear.   What! art mad? A man may see how this world goes with
        no eyes. Look with thine ears: see how yond justice rails
        upon yond simple thief. Hark, in thine ear: change places,
        and, handy-dandy, which is the justice, which is the thief?
        Thou hast seen a farmer's dog bark at a beggar?
Gloucester.   Ay, Sir.
Lear.   And the creature run from the cur? There thou might'st
        behold
        The great image of Authority:
        A dog's obey'd in office.
        Thou rascal beadle, hold thy bloody hand!
        Why dost thou lash that whore? Strip thine own back;
        Thou hotly lusts to use her in that kind
        For which thou whipp'st her. The usurer hangs the
        cozener.
        Through tatter'd clothes small vices do appear;
        Robes and furr'd gowns hide all. Plate sin with gold,
        And the strong lance of justice hurtless breaks;
        Arm it in rags, a pigmy's straw does pierce it.
        None does offend, none, I say, none; I'll able 'em.

'None does offend, none, I say, none; I'll able 'em.' That last
line shares the ambiguity of so many of the pronouncements

---

[1] *Some Shakespearean Themes*, p. 105.

made in this play. 'None does offend' because we are all as bad as each other. That is one sense. But because at more than one point Lear has now admitted his own guilt and involvement, there is a bridge to the second sense: 'none does offend' because at the most fundamental level of all no one has a right to condemn. And what is held in tension is not only two senses but two basic attitudes—utter revulsion ('Give me an ounce of civet, good apothecary, To sweeten my imagination'), on the one hand: on the other an unconditional and unquestioning charity, of the kind that had allowed Cordelia to invoke the unpublished virtues of the earth as remedies for 'the good man's distress', the good man being of course the erring Lear. Naturally, as we watch or read, we do not debate these alternatives as an abstract issue: we are simply carried forward—alert and engaged—to the immediately succeeding scene where this and other issues are resolved in terms of the awakened imagination.

> *Lear.* Do not laugh at me;
>   For as I am a man, I think this lady
>   To be my child Cordelia.
> *Cordelia.* And so I am, I am.
> *Lear.* Be your tears wet? Yes, faith. I pray, weep not:
>   If you have poison for me, I will drink it.
>   I know you do not love me; for your sisters
>   Have, as I do remember, done me wrong:
>   You have some cause, they have not.
> *Cordelia.* No cause, no cause.

It is subtly done. Lear's thoughts, as he comes to himself in his daughter's presence, are still on punishment for his sins, on the weighing of retribution against offence. It is with four words that Cordelia brushes aside all forms of proportionate justice and reveals a justice of an utterly different kind. It is, I suppose, what Paul Tillich would call reconciling or transforming justice, which can help a man to become what he is and what his nature most deeply craves.[1] Clearly this raises the whole question of man's nature and the wider 'nature' with which he finds himself involved: and indeed within the *Lear* world the line of thought we have been following has been developed in the context of these wider questions. Here we will simply notice that within that context the question of Justice has been lifted to a plane transcending that of our everyday conceptions. Not of course that we are left with a new concept. It is simply that in the upward surge of the metaphoric process a new direction for imaginative thought appears. Rooted in the given instance—in the highly complex metaphor that *King Lear* is—it unfolds, and goes on unfolding, in our own lives. In a sense we live the metaphors we have assimilated.

In *The Transformation of Nature in Art* Ananda Coomaraswamy glosses the term *yün* as used by a Chinese writer on aesthetics: 'The idea *yün*, of operation or reverberation, is strictly comparable to what is meant by the *dhvani* of Indian rhetoricians, it being only as it were by an echoing in the heart of the hearer that the full meaning of a word (or any other symbol) can be realized.' *Dhvani*, he adds, 'is literally "sound", especially sound like that of thunder or a drum, hence "resonance" or "overtone" of meaning'—i.e. the verbal noun 'sounding', rather than the noun 'sound'.[2] I am ignorant of Chinese and Indian aesthetics, but it seems to me that this comment throws light on the metaphoric process we have been considering. Martin Foss, you will recall, speaks of this as 'a process of tension and energy'. The tension, as we have seen in *King Lear*, is the apprehension of meanings somehow held in relation to each other, and to a central drive of interest, so that each meaning is more clearly defined in relation to the others, and what I have called the drive of interest is established in a certain direction.

[1] See Paul Tillich, *Love, Power and Justice.*
[2] Ananda Coomaraswamy, *The Transformation of Nature in Art* (New York: Dover Publications), pp. 187, 198.

The energy is an energy of understanding. It is of course obvious that more than the conceptual understanding is involved; it is only through the reader's imagination responding to the imagination of the poet (bringing 'the whole soul of man into activity') that the work becomes alive. But the point I am making is that the imagination thus conceived is an instrument of knowledge—not 'knowledge of' something fixed and definite, but knowledge as a 'sounding', 'an echoing in the heart of the hearer'.

It is in the hope of elucidating this process that I have examined some small part of *King Lear*. The play is not just a symbolic form in which modes of feeling are held before us for contemplation. It is a moving image of life, in the sense not of course that it merely affects our feelings, but that it sets in motion those powers of apprehension through which we simultaneously become aware of, and make, our world.

The Question of Character in
Shakespeare

LET me begin with an unashamed bit of autobiography. In
1932 I was asked to give a paper to the Shakespeare Association in London. I was a comparatively young man, dissatisfied
with the prevailing academic approach to Shakespeare, excited
by the glimpses I had obtained of new and, it seemed, more
rewarding approaches, and I welcomed the opportunity of
proclaiming the new principles in the very home of Shakespearean orthodoxy, whilst at the same time having some fun with
familiar irrelevancies of the kind parodied in my title, *How Many
Children had Lady Macbeth?* I gave my paper and waited expec-
tantly for the lively discussion that would follow this rousing
challenge to the pundits. So far as I remember, nothing happened, except that after a period of silence an elderly man got up
at the back of the room and said that he was very glad to hear
Mr Knights give this paper because it was what he had always
thought. The revolution was over, and I went home. It was
hardly a historic occasion, and the only reason for mentioning
it is that when my paper was published as one of Gordon Fraser's
Minority Pamphlets it obtained a certain mild notoriety that
has never since entirely deserted it: only a few years ago a writer
in *The Listener* called it 'the Communist Manifesto of the new
critical movement'. Well of course it was nothing of the kind.
How Many Children had Lady Macbeth? has earned its footnote
in the history of modern criticism partly, I like to believe,
because it says a few sensible things about *Macbeth*, partly
because of its sprightly title (which was suggested to me by F. R.
Leavis), and partly because it reflected the conviction of an
increasing number of readers that the prevailing language of
Shakespeare criticism didn't quite fit what seemed to them of

deepest importance in the experience of Shakespeare's plays. In the last twenty-five or thirty years there has certainly been a movement away from the older type of 'character' criticism which had for so long held the field and which culminated in A. C. Bradley's *Shakespearean Tragedy*. But so far as any one book can be said to have heralded the new movement it was G. Wilson Knight's *The Wheel of Fire* (1930), shortly to be followed by *The Imperial Theme* (1931).

Now what I am here to do today is to try to get one aspect of that movement into perspective; more specifically I want to ask, after some twenty-five years of Shakespeare criticism that has not on the whole been on Bradleyean lines, what we now understand by the term 'character' when we use it in giving an account of Shakespeare's plays, to what extent—and within what limitations—'character' can be a useful critical term when we set out to define the meaning—the living and life-nourishing significance—of a Shakespeare play.

I don't want to burden you with a history of Shakespeare criticism, ancient or modern, but a few historical reminders are necessary. Since Shakespeare criticism began, people have praised Shakespeare for the lifelikeness of his characters. But it was not until the end of the eighteenth century that Shakespeare's remarkable power to make his men and women convincing led to a more and more exclusive concentration on those features of the *dramatis personae* that could be defined in terms appropriate to characters in real life. The *locus classicus* is of course Maurice Morgann's *Essay on the Dramatic Character of Sir John Falstaff* (1777). Twelve years before, in 1765, Dr Johnson, in his great Preface, had given the more traditional view:

> Nothing can please many, and please long, but just representations of general nature. . . . Shakespeare is above all writers, at least above all modern writers, the poet of nature. . . . His persons act and speak by the influence of those general passions and prin-

ciples by which all minds are agitated, and the whole system of life is continued in motion. In the writings of other poets a character is too often an individual; in those of Shakespeare it is commonly a species.

It is from this wide extension of design that so much instruction is derived. . . .[1]

Morgann, on the contrary, is interested in what is uniquely individual in the character he describes, and these individual traits, he affirms, can be elicited from the stage characters in much the same way as one builds up the character of an acquaintance in real life: 'those characters in Shakespeare, which are seen only in part, are yet capable of being unfolded and understood in the whole'.

If the characters of Shakespeare [he goes on] are thus *whole*, and as it were original, while those of almost all other writers are mere imitation, it may be fit to consider them rather as Historic than Dramatic beings; and, when occasion requires, to account for their conduct from the *whole* of character, from general principles, from latent motives, and from policies not avowed.

It is this principle that allows him to distinguish between 'the *real* character of Falstaff' and 'his *apparent* one'. What R. W. Babcock, in his useful book, *The Genesis of Shakespeare Idolatry, 1766–99*, calls 'the psychologizing of Shakespeare' was well established even before Coleridge gave his lectures; and Coleridge's influence, though of course more subtly, worked in the same direction. It seems true to say that in the nineteenth century Shakespeare's characters became 'real people', and—

[1] We may compare Johnson's characteristic comment on *Macbeth*: 'The play is deservedly celebrated for the propriety of its fictions, and solemnity, grandeur, and variety of its action; but it has no nice discriminations of character, the events are too great to admit the influence of particular dispositions, and the course of the action necessarily determines the conduct of the agents. The danger of ambition is well described. . . .' Johnson, it is true, also says of Shakespeare, 'Perhaps no poet ever kept his personages more distinct from each other.'

with varying degrees of relevance—the plays were discussed in terms of the interaction of real people for whom sympathy or antipathy was enlisted. Bradley's tremendously influential *Shakespearean Tragedy* was published in 1904, and for Bradley 'the centre of the tragedy . . . may be said with equal truth to lie in action issuing from character, or in character issuing in action': 'action is the centre of the story', but 'this action is essentially the expression of character'.

Now Bradley had the great virtue of being thoroughly immersed in what he was talking about, and I am sure that his book has helped very many people to make Shakespeare a present fact in their lives. Also there is no need to make Bradley responsible for all the vagaries of the how-many-children-had-Lady-Macbeth? kind, which mostly lie on the fringes of criticism. But Bradley's book did endorse a particular kind of preoccupation with 'character', and once 'character'-criticism became the dominant mode of approach to Shakespeare, certain important matters were necessarily obscured, and people's experience of Shakespeare became in some ways less rich and satisfying than it might have been. For one thing genuine perceptions became entangled with irrelevant speculations—'How is it that Othello comes to be the companion of the one man in the world, who is at once able enough, brave enough, and vile enough to ensnare him?'; Macbeth's tendency to ambition 'must have been greatly strengthened by his marriage'. And if the critic who accepts too naïvely the character-in-action formula is liable to disappear down by-paths outside the play, he is almost equally likely to slight or ignore what is actually there if it does not minister to his particular preoccupation—witness the ease with which the old Arden edition of *Macbeth* dismissed as spurious scenes that do not contribute to the development of character or of a narrowly conceived dramatic action. Even at its best the focus is a narrow one. Shakespearean tragedy, says Bradley, 'is pre-eminently the story of one person, the "hero", or at most of two, the "hero" and "heroine" '; and the mark of the tragic hero, besides his greatness, is that there is a 'conflict of forces' in his soul. I suppose, if you look at matters in this way it doesn't necessarily mean that you idealize the hero as Bradley does Othello, missing the critical 'placing' determined by the play as a whole. But it does mean that you are likely to ignore some important matters, such as the structure of ideas in *Macbeth*. After all, in his greater plays, Shakespeare was doing more than merely holding a mirror up to nature, more even than representing conflict in the souls of mighty characters: he was exploring the world and defining the values by which men live. In short, Shakespearean tragedy, any Shakespearean tragedy, is saying so much more than can be expressed in Bradleyan terms. It was some such perceptions as these—combined with an increasing knowledge of Elizabethan dramatic usage and convention—that prompted exploration of Shakespeare, not necessarily in opposition to Bradley, but to a large extent outside the Bradleyan frame of reference.

Simplifying for the sake of clarity, I would say that as a result of critical work done in the last quarter of a century, the approach to Shakespeare of an intelligent and informed reader today is likely to differ in three important respects from that of the intelligent and informed reader of a generation ago. To start with, he is likely to take it for granted that any one of Shakespeare's greater plays is very much more than a dramatized story; that it is, rather, a vision of life—more or less complex and inclusive—whose meaning is nothing less than the *play as a whole*. This is what Wilson Knight meant when he sometimes referred to his work in terms of 'spatial analysis', as distinguished from the analysis of a series of steps in time. Ideally, we try to apprehend each play as though all its parts were simultaneously present: there is an obvious analogy with music, and criticism of this kind tends to describe Shakespeare's meanings in terms of 'themes' rather than in terms of motive, character-development, and so on. Wilson Knight speaks of cutting below 'the surface crust of plot and character', and remarks that in *Macbeth*, for example, 'the logic of imaginative correspondence is more significant and more exact than the logic of plot'. He also, of course, told us that 'we should not look for perfect verisimilitude to life, but rather see each play as an expanded metaphor, by means of which the original vision has been projected into forms roughly correspondent with actuality'; and the fact that this remark has been quoted in innumerable examination papers shouldn't obscure its crucial importance in determining the kind of approach to Shakespeare that I am trying to define.[1] In the second place, our contemporary reader is likely to take for granted that the essential structure of the plays is to be sought in the poetry rather than in the more easily extractable elements of 'plot' and 'character'. I think our age is more aware of the complex structure, of the depth of life, of Shakespeare's verse, than any of its predecessors. Critics have written at length about his imagery, his ambiguities and overlaying meanings, his word-play, and so on; and there is no doubt that such studies have sharpened our sense not only of the tremendous activity of Shakespeare's verse—its generative power—but of the strong and subtle interconnexions of meaning within the imaginative structure of the plays. It is significant that 'interpretation' relies heavily on extensive quotation and detailed analysis.[2] Finally—abandoning my hypothetical intelligent reader—I should say that our whole conception of Shakespeare's relation to his work,

---

[1] 'And Shakespeare's was a mind that thought in images, so that metaphor packs into metaphor, producing the most surprising collocations of apparently diverse phenomena; he thought of time, and death, and eternity, in terms of a candle, a shadow, and an actor. Is it not likely that the large and composite image of the story as a whole would serve him as a metaphor or symbol for his attitudes to certain aspects of experience?'—S. L. Bethell, *Shakespeare and the Popular Dramatic Tradition*, p. 115.

[2] A method that has its dangers, for we sometimes seem to run the risk of having the play read for us.

of what he was trying to do as an artist whilst at the same time satisfying the demands of the Elizabethan theatre, has undergone a very great change indeed. The 'new' Shakespeare, I should say, is much less impersonal than the old. Whereas in the older view Shakespeare was the god-like creator of a peopled world, projecting—it is true—his own spirit into the inhabitants, but remaining essentially the analyst of 'their' passions, he is now felt as much more immediately engaged in the action he puts before us. I don't of course mean that we have returned to Frank Harris's Shakespeare, engaged in drawing a succession of full-length portraits of himself, but that we feel the plays (in Mr Eliot's words) 'to be united by one significant, consistent, and developing personality': we feel that the plays, even if 'in no obvious form', 'are somehow dramatizing . . . an action or struggle for harmony in the soul of the poet.'[1] We take it for granted that Shakespeare thought about the problems of life, and was at least as much interested in working towards an imaginative solution as he was in making a series of detached studies of different characters, their motives and their passions. Here again, specialist studies are indicative: we think it reasonable that a scholar should inquire what evidence there is that Shakespeare had read Hooker, and if so what effect it had on his plays; we inquire into Shakespeare's political ideas and their background; we are prepared to examine *Shakespeare's Philosophical Patterns* (which is the title of a book by the American scholar, W. C. Curry). In short, we take seriously Coleridge's remark that Shakespeare was 'a philosopher'; the vision of life that his plays express is, in a certain sense, a philosophic vision. But at the same time we remember—at least, I should like to be able to say we remember—that the plays are not dramatizations of abstract ideas, but imaginative constructions mediated through the poetry. If Shakespeare's verse has moved well into the centre of the picture, one reasom is that linguistic vitality is

[1] See T. S. Eliot's essay on John Ford.

now felt as the chief clue to the urgent personal themes that not only shape the poetic-dramatic structure of each play but form the figure in the carpet of the canon as a whole.[1]

This short and imperfect account may serve as an indication or reminder of the main lines of Shakespeare criticism since 1930, or thereabouts. Happily my job is not to award marks of merit to different critics, and I don't intend to offer a list of obligatory reading. We all have our own ideas about the recent critics who have helped us most in our understanding of Shakespeare, and I don't suppose that we should all agree about all of them. But I think we should agree that there have been some books offering genuinely new insights, and that where criticism has been most illuminating it has usually been on quite non-Bradleyean lines. At the same time let us recall certain facts. If 'plot' and 'character'—mere 'precipitates from the memory'—sometimes seem to be described in abstraction from the full living immediacy of our direct experience of the plays, and therefore to lead away from it, so too 'themes' and 'symbols' can be pursued mechanically and, as it were, abstractly. Whereas it is equally obvious that criticism in terms of 'character' can be genuinely revealing; John Palmer's *The Political Characters of Shakespeare* is an example. And of course you can't get away from the term. Not only does the ordinary theatregoer or reader need it to explain his enjoyment, but even critics least in sympathy with Bradley at times naturally and necessarily define their sense of significance in terms appropriate to living people. Clearly the critical field has not been given over to those whom J. I. M. Stewart calls 'the new Bowdlers, whom man delights not, no nor woman neither, and who would give us not merely *Hamlet* without the Prince but the Complete Works without their several *dramatis personae*'. The notion of 'character', in some sense, has not disappeared, and is not going to disappear, from Shakespeare

[1] A few sentences in this paragraph are borrowed from *Some Shakespearean Themes*.

criticism. What we need to do is simply to clear up our minds about it, to make our handling of the term both more flexible and more precise.

Before I give my own simple summing up of things as I see them I should like to mention two books that have a direct bearing on the matters we are pursuing. The first is J. I. M. Stewart's witty, entertaining and instructive *Character and Motive in Shakespeare*. Stewart not only has some shrewd knocks at those who over-play the element of Elizabethan dramatic convention in Shakespeare and those who would tailor the plays too closely to the pattern of their own proprieties, he has some illuminating comments on particular plays. But his main interest, in the present connexion, lies in the way he develops the conception of character-presentation beyond the bounds of naturalism. To the extent that Shakespeare is concerned with character and motive—and he does 'present "man" and reveal psychological truths'—he works not through realistic portrayal but through poetry—that is, through symbolism and suggestion as well as by more direct means; and in this way he makes us aware not—or not only—of what we normally understand by character but of its hidden recesses.

> The characters, then (but I mean chiefly those major characters with whom the imagination of the dramatist is deeply engaged), have often the superior reality of individuals exposing the deepest springs of their action. But this superior reality is manifested through the medium of situations which are sometimes essentially symbolical; and these may be extravagant or merely fantastic when not interpreted by the quickened imagination, for it is only during the prevalence of a special mode of consciousness, the poetic, that the underlying significance of these situations is perceived. (pp. 9–10)

> Of just what Shakespeare brings from beyond this portal [of the depths of the mind], and how, we often can achieve little con-

ceptual grasp; and often therefore the logical and unkindled mind finds difficulties which it labels as faults and attributes to the depravity of Shakespeare's audience or what it wills. But what the intellect finds arbitrary the imagination may accept and respond to, for when we read imaginatively or poetically we share the dramatist's penetration for a while and deep is calling to deep. (p. 30)[1]

The other book I want to refer to is *Character and Society in Shakespeare* by Professor Arthur Sewell. It is a small book but, I think, an important one. Briefly, Mr Sewell's contention is that the characters of a play only exist within the total vision that the play presents: 'in Shakespeare's plays the essential process of character-creation is a prismatic breaking-up of the comprehensive vision of the play' (p. 19). There is, therefore, an absolute

---

[1] This insistence on the imaginative—on the non-rational but not therefore irrational—portrayal of character, and on the need to respond to it imaginatively, is important, and, as I have said, Mr Stewart can be illuminating. But it also seems to me that his method, as he pursues it, can sometimes lead outside the play, as in his use of psycho-analytic concepts to define Leontes' jealousy. The main criticism of any psycho-analytic account of Shakespeare's characters is not simply that it is irrelevant—though it may be —but that it reduces the material it works on to a category that can be known and docketed. To accept it is to feel that you know about a character something of importance that has been simply handed over, and that can be received alike by every reader, whatever the degree of his concern, the extent of his actual engagement, with the plays. It obscures not only the uniqueness but the *activity* of the work of art; whereas any play only exists for you to the extent that *you* have grappled with its meanings. Thus Mr Stewart's account of Leontes' repressed homosexuality (reactivated by the presence of Polixenes, and then 'projected' on to Hermione) is relevant inasmuch as it points to the presence in what Leontes stands for of unconscious motivations, of motives beyond conscious control. But within the context of the play as a whole their exact nature is irrelevant: they are simply an X within the equation which is the play. What the play gives us is the awakening of new life that can enlist the same impulses which, in the first part, have been shown as the material of an unruly aberration. All we need to know of the aberration is that it is a representative manifestation: to pin it down exactly as Mr Stewart does, is to make Leontes' jealousy something that we *know about* instead of something we *respond to* as part of the total generative pattern of the play.

distinction between a dramatic character and a person in real life whose conduct can be accounted for 'from general principles, from latent motives, and from policies not avowed'. 'We can only understand Shakespeare's characters so long as we agree that we cannot know all about them and are not supposed to know all about them' (p. 12). What is relevant for us is not an assumed hinterland of motives but simply the particular 'address to the world' that is embodied, with different degrees of explicitness, in the different characters. In the comedies the characters tend to be static and, so to speak, socially conditioned: they represent attitudes and modes of judgment that serve for the presentation and critical inspection of our everyday world. In the great tragedies the characters speak from out of a deeper level of experience—'metaphysical' rather than social, though the distinction is not absolute; the vision they embody is transformed in the full working out of the attitudes to which they are committed; and their reality is established by our own active commitment to the drama's dialectical play. Of both comedy and tragedy it can be said that 'unless Shakespeare had set our minds busy—and not only our minds—on various kinds of evaluation, his characters could never have engaged us and would have lacked all vitality' (p. 18). And again, there is the suggestion 'that character and moral vision must be apprehended together, and that when character is understood separately from moral vision it is not in fact understood at all' (p. 59).

Where, then, at the end of all this, do we come out? Perhaps only among what many people will regard as a handful of commonplaces. Let me start with the most thumping platitude of all: in Shakespeare's plays *some* impression of character is constantly being made upon us. It is likely to begin as soon as a major character is introduced.

> Why, I, in this weak piping time of peace,
> Have no delight to pass away the time,

> Unless to see my shadow in the sun
> And descant on mine own deformity.
>
> Though yet of Hamlet our dear brother's death
> The memory be green, and that it us befitted
> To bear our hearts in grief and our whole kingdom
> To be contracted in one brow of woe,
> Yet so far hath discretion fought with nature. . . .

> I pray you, daughter, sing; or express yourself in a more comfortable sort.

Here, and in innumerable other instances, we have what Mr Sewell calls the 'distillation of personality into style'. We know these people by the way they speak; as Mr Stewart puts it, 'In drama the voice *is* the character'—though we also have to add that often Shakespeare speaks *through* the person with a meaning different from, or even contrary to, that apparently intended by the speaker.

At the same time we have to admit that our sense of character —of a complex, unified tissue of thought and feeling from which a particular voice issues—varies enormously not only as between different plays, but as between the different figures within a single play. *All's Well That Ends Well* is nearer to a morality play, and is less concerned with characterization, in any sense, than is *Othello*. In *Measure for Measure* 'analysis of character' may take us a long way with Angelo; it is utterly irrelevant as applied to the Duke.

Let me give another example—which will serve to illustrate Mr Sewell's remark about the characters embodying 'an address to the world', in case anyone should have been left uneasy with that phrase. Here is Don John introducing himself in conversation with Conrade in Act I of *Much Ado About Nothing*.

> I wonder that thou, being—as thou say'st thou art—born under
> Saturn, goest about to apply a moral medicine to a mortifying

mischief. I cannot hide what I am: I must be sad when I have cause, and smile at no man's jests; eat when I have stomach, and wait for no man's leisure; sleep when I am drowsy, and tend on no man's business; laugh when I am merry, and claw no man in his humour.

Conrade advises that he should apply himself to winning the good opinion of his brother the Duke, with whom he is lately reconciled, and Don John goes on:

I had rather be a canker in a hedge than a rose in his grace; and it better fits my blood to be disdained of all than to fashion a carriage to rob love from any: in this, though I cannot be said to be a flattering honest man, it must not be denied but I am a plain-dealing villain. I am trusted with a muzzle and enfranchised with a clog; therefore I have decreed not to sing in my cage. If I had my mouth, I would bite; if I had my liberty, I would do my liking: in the meantime, let me be that I am, and seek not to alter me.

A good many things are plain from this—Don John's exacerbated sense of superiority ('I...I...I...'), his particular kind of 'melancholy', and his affectation of a blunt, no-nonsense manner. Clearly he is related to Richard of Gloucester and to Iago. Their common characteristic is an egotism that clenches itself hard against the claims of sympathy, and that is unwilling to change—'I cannot hide what I am; I must be sad when I have cause ... let me be that I am, and seek not to alter me.' It is, in short, the opposite of a character 'open' to others and to the real demands of the present. That is all we know about Don John and all we are required to know: we are not asked to consider his bastardy or his other grievances. He is simply a perversely 'melancholy' man who serves as villain of the piece, the agent of an otherwise unmotivated evil.

What is true of a minor figure like Don John is true of all the characters of Shakespeare: we know about them only what the play requires us to know. Even to put the matter in this way is—as we shall see in a minute—over-simplified and misleading, but it serves to remind us that however we define for ourselves a character and his rôle, there is a strict criterion of relevance: he belongs to his play, and his play is an art-form, not a slice of life. The fact that this at least is now a commonplace is a guarantee that we shall never again have to waste our time on the complete irrelevance of some forms of character-analysis as applied to Shakespeare's *dramatis personae*.

But we still haven't got to the heart of the matter. What is the 'play as a whole', to which we say the characters are subordinate? To this question there is no simple answer, but we can at least attempt an answer that will help our reading.

Poetic drama offers a vision of life, more or less complex, more or less wide-embracing. Shakespeare's poetic drama as a whole is different from Jonson's or Racine's; and within Shakespeare's poetic drama as a whole there are many different kinds. Even at its simplest there is some degree of complexity, of dialectical play, as persons embodying different attitudes are set before us in action and interaction. Of course when we are watching them we don't think of them as them ebodiment of attitudes—of different addresses to the world: we say simply, Rosalind is in love with Orlando. Yet while we know that two addresses to the world can't fall in love, we also know —and this knowledge moves from the back of our minds and comes into action when, having seen or read the play several times, we try to bring it into sharper focus—that Shakespeare is doing something more significant with Rosalind and Orlando than showing us how interesting it is when boy meets girl. *As You Like It*, which is a fairly simple play, will help us here. *As You Like It* is of course a romantic comedy, with its own interest and entertainment as such. But the plot and the structure of the incidents point to an interest in the meaning of a life lived 'according to nature'. Duke Senior's idyllic picture ('Hath not

old custom made this life more sweet Than that of painted pomp?'
etc.) is an over-simplification, as the play makes plain; but it is
a possible attitude, put forward for inspection, and as the play
goes on it is clear that we are meant to take an intelligent interest
in the varying degrees of naturalness and sophistication—each
playing off against the other—that are put before us. *As You
Like It*, in short, rings the changes on the contrasting meanings
of 'natural' (either 'human' or 'close down to the life of nature')
and 'civilized' (either 'well nurtured' or 'artificial')—all especially pointed with reference to the passion of love. It is largely
an entertainment; but at the same time it is a serious comedy of
ideas—not abstract ideas to be debated, but ideas as embodied
in attitude and action. So that by playing off against each other
different attitudes to life, the play as a whole offers a criticism
of various forms of exaggeration and affectation—either 'romantic' or professedly realistic—with Rosalind as arbiter, although of course she is not above the action but involved in
it herself.[1]

What is true of *As You Like It* is also true of greater plays, such
as *Measure for Measure*, *King Lear*, or *Antony and Cleopatra*,
though in these of course the play of varied sympathies and anti-
pathies, of imaginative evaluation as different possibilities of
living are put before us, is more complex, and the experience
handled is more profound. But of all the greater plays it is true
to say that *all* the characters are necessary to express the vision—
the emergent 'idea' or controlling preoccupation—and they are
necessary only in so far as they do express it. Gloucester's part
in *King Lear* is not to give additional human interest, but to
enact and express a further aspect of the Lear experience; for
with Gloucester, as with Lear, confident acceptance of an
inadequate code gives place to humble acceptance of the human
condition, and there are glimpses of a new wisdom:

[1] See James Smith's excellent essay on *As You Like It* in *Scrutiny*,
IX, i.

> I have no way, and therefore want no eyes;
> I stumbled when I saw.

The striking parallels between the two men are proof enough of deliberate artistic intention in this respect.

What *King Lear* also forces on us, even when we are prepared to see the different characters as contributing to a pattern, is the inadequacy of terms relating to 'character'. What character has Edgar in his successive transformations? In the storm scenes, where Lear's vision of horror is built to a climax, we are acted on directly by the poetry, by what is said, in some respects independently of our sense of a particular person saying it. So too in the play as a whole, and in the other greater plays, our sense of the characters—of what the characters stand for in their 'address to the world', their 'moral encounter with the universe' —is inseparable from the more direct ways in which, by poetry and symbolism, our imaginations are called into play. To take one simple example. When Macbeth, on his first appearance, says, 'So foul and fair a day I have not seen', he does far more than announce himself as a character—tired, collected, brooding; echoing the Witches' 'Fair is foul, and foul is fair', he takes his place in the pattern of moral evaluations which make the play so much more than the story of a tragic hero, which make it into a great vision of the unreality, the negative horror, that evil is. In reading Shakespeare our sense of 'character', defined and limited as I have tried to define and limit it, is important; but so is our responsiveness to symbolism (the storm in *Othello* and Othello's trance, Lear's bare heath and Gloucester's Dover Cliff, Hermione's moving statue), and so is our responsiveness to imagery (the imagery of darkness conveying spiritual blindness in *Macbeth*), to verse rhythm, and to all the inter-acting elements of the poetry: it is from these that there emerges a controlling direction of exploratory and committed interests—of interests involving the personality as a whole—that we indicate by some such word as 'themes'.

Mr John Holloway has recently objected to the use of 'theme' in Shakespeare criticism[1]: it is a sign that the work in question is to be reduced to a generalized moral reflection, whereas literature does not provide us with general truths, only with particular instances. 'What *Macbeth* does ... is to depict for us, in great and remarkable detail, one imagined case and one only.' 'Narrative', he suggests, is 'the fundamental quality of the full-length work', the essential principle of imaginative order. Now both these conceptions of the work of art as 'one imagined case and one only', and of 'narrative' as the controlling principle, seem to me to be, in their turn, open to objection. But I think we are dealing with something far greater than the particular question —Is Shakespeare most profitably discussed in terms of 'character' or 'theme' or 'narrative'? What has come into sight, what we must take account of, is nothing less than the depth of life of any great work of art, its capacity to enter into our lives as power. What do we mean when we say that a great work of art has a universal appeal? Surely something more than that it tells a story likely to interest everybody. We mean that the special case (and I grant Mr Holloway the artist's 'passion for the special case') brings to a focus a whole range of awareness, that it generates an activity of imaginative apprehension that illuminates not only the 'case' in question but life as we know it in our own experience: it can modify, or even transform, our whole way of seeing life and responding to it. It is this capacity to generate meanings that is the 'universal' quality in the particular work of art. And it is the presence of the universal in the particular that compels the use of such generalizing terms as 'themes' or 'motifs'. Of course, like other critical terms, they can be used mechanically or ineptly, can harden into counters pushed about in a critical game. But as simple pointers their function is to indicate the *direction* of interest that a play compels when we

[1] 'The New "Establishment" in Criticism', *The Listener*, September 20 and 27, 1956; more recently developed in his book, *The Story of the Night*.

try to meet it with the whole of ourselves—to meet it, that is (using De Quincey's term), as literature of power.

To read Shakespeare, then (and in reading I include seeing his plays performed), we need to cultivate a complex skill. But there is no need to make heavy weather of this. That skill can be largely intuitive; we can obtain it in many ways, and there is no need (especially if we are teachers) to be too insistent on any one approach. In 'Demosius and Mystes', a dialogue appended to *Church and State*, Coleridge refers to a mighty conflict between two cats, 'where one tail alone is said to have survived the battle'. There is always a danger of critical squabbles becoming like that; and I for one would rather see among my pupils an honest and first-hand appreciation of what is offered by way of 'character' than a merely mechanical working out of recurrent imagery and symbolic situations. We should remember also that the life of the imagination runs deeper than our conscious formulations. T. S. Eliot (in his Introduction to S. L. Bethell's book on Shakespeare), says of the persons of the play of a modern verse dramatist,

> they must on your stage be able to perform the same actions, and lead the same lives, as in the real world. But they must somehow disclose (not necessarily be aware of) a deeper reality than that of the plane of most of our conscious living; and what they disclose must be, not the psychologist's intellectualization of this reality, but the reality itself.

They must 'somehow disclose (not necessarily be aware of) a deeper reality': I think that what Eliot says of the persons in verse plays like his own, applies—*mutatis mutandis*—to the spectators of poetic drama. To the extent that a Shakespeare tragedy truly enlists the imagination (and this means enlisting it for what is in the play, not for a display of virtuosity) it is precisely this deeper level of apprehension—the hidden potentialities, wishes, and fears of the individual spectator—that is being worked on, even though the spectator himself may not be conscious of it, and thinks that he is simply watching someone else's 'character issuing in action'.

All the same, even when this is admitted, there is no reason why the common reader should not be encouraged to see rather more. For it is in our imaginative response to *the whole play*—not simply to what can be extracted as 'character', nor indeed to what can be simply extracted as 'theme' or 'symbol' —that the meaning lies; and Shakespeare calls on us to be as fully conscious as we can, even if consciousness includes relaxed enjoyment and absorption as well as, sometimes, more deliberate attention to this or that aspect of the whole experience.